Silent, Fragile
and Isolated

Each of us now an island:

threats to our conversation,

intellect and national solidarity

Philippe Jaquenod

i

A catalogue record for this
book is available from the
National Library of Australia

Linellen Press
265 Boomerang Road
Oldbury, Western Australia
www.linellenpress.com.au

'Let us build wisely, let us build surely, let us build faithfully, let us build not for the moment, but for the years that are to come, and to establish here below what we hope to find above- a house of many mansions where there shall be room for all' (Winston Churchill)

Acknowledgments

To my wife M, for her constant patience and endurance during the many hours when I isolated myself in the office to write this manuscript, and also for her proofreading of this work and invaluable practical input and wisdom in our life journey together.

To my friend H.D for making so many excellent suggestions, amendments and amplifications to the rough copy of this publication.

To Professor Augusto Zimmerman, Professor & Head of Law, Sheridan Institute of Higher Education, Perth, Western Australia for his encouragement and review of the contents of the original manuscript. Naturally, I take sole and full responsibility for the final manuscript.

To a wonderful young couple, B & R, for their friendship and love and readiness to build up relationships with persons espousing a different worldview.

To all my friends, family members and acquaintances (you know who you are) for their interest and encouragement in my work.

Contents

Introduction

Come Now, Let Us Reason Together

'If the freedom of speech is taken away, then dumb and silent may we be led, like sheep to the slaughter.'

(George Washington)

French-born, I came to Australia some fifty years ago with an inquisitive mind. A fully bilingual qualified Commercial Translator, I was interested in finding out what this 'new country' had to offer.

I came out of curiosity. I came initially for two years and then eventually took up the Australian citizenship and stayed for a lifetime.

France has a rich cultural background and a long history; it has been the cradle of some great thinkers, artists and writers but I was intrigued by what Australia had to offer.

New opportunities, an easier lifestyle, a sense of adventure all contributed to a feeling of excitement, foundational to the decision to migrate.

In retrospect, my life in Australia turned out to be very different from what, in all likelihood, it would have been had I stayed in France, instead of migrating to these shores as a newlywed Frenchman.

In hindsight, I think the decision to migrate and stay was an extremely sound one. I managed to complete my university education in Australia; I founded a family and succeeded in

1

occupying a number of senior positions that most likely would not have been available to me in Europe.

Most importantly, I found a faith and value system which was somewhat lacking in 1970's France.

But now, I am concerned as I feel that much of what has been achieved in the past is on the verge of being lost.

I am concerned because I believe that we, Australians, are losing the art of communication. We have also lost interest in learning and in peaceful debating.

I perceive that we are on the verge of being more introverted, more timid, more hesitant in our written and oral expression.

I perceive that we have now become less interested in what others might think or feel and, at the same time, more sensitive to criticism.

Admittedly, many of us love to hear what others have to say but only if they say what we want to hear. For this reason, I do not believe that the message of this book will be welcomed by all.

I expect many will consider this book controversial and, if this is the case, my objective will have been met: I am keen to see ideas being honestly and freely debated by all.

There is, however, no malice in my writing but only a loving concern.

It is important that I state at the outset of this work that I do not harbour any ill feelings, let alone hatred, towards anybody or towards any segment of the population or to those who have adopted a different lifestyle than mine. Nevertheless, I am very concerned by some of the directions our Australian society is embarking upon.

I am not concerned so much about myself as I have now entered what the French euphemistically call '*le troisième âge*' (loosely translated: the third part of a lifetime) and what we, Australians, more bluntly refer to as 'the elderly population'.

No, instead I am concerned for my children but, more particularly, for my grandchildren and the generations yet to come.

This loss in communication skills in our society at large will have significant impacts on intellectual and spiritual life. Intellectually, there cannot be any further advance that is not preceded by debate and a free and honest exchange of views.

In Australia, in the middle of the last century, the slogan 'populate or perish' was broadcast regularly in order to stress the importance of immigration. Immigration at the time was considered an essential ingredient of our sustained viability, both culturally and economically.

Nowadays, we should start a new mantra: "Communicate or perish!"

Without free exchange of thoughts, we will all perish intellectually and spiritually. If only one viewpoint, one world view is acceptable, then all belief systems which depart from it will be repressed and persecuted. Totalitarian regimes are proof of this.

I do not wish to be alarmist and argue that Australia is now a totalitarian state, but nevertheless, we should all be aware of the increasing limitations placed on our freedom of expression. Many are already scared and afraid to speak. Many now choose the path of avoidance and have decided to isolate themselves socially.

We have become **silent, fragile and isolated**.

We are **silent** because we are increasingly being silenced by the media (and particularly social media) and by the woke elites[1] (aka the universities, big business, the New Left); we are **fragile**

---

[1] Woke is a slang term now commonly used in New Left circles to describe those who are presumably more conscious (i.e., more awake) of the so-called cultural injustices perpetrated by Western nations in the past and in the present.

because we are increasingly traumatised by how others are going to misinterpret our words; we are **isolated** as we increasingly choose to avoid traumatic confrontations.

We are being drowned in a culture of victimhood where anybody can claim to be offended by anything we say or do.

A new word has emerged: microaggression.

We are concerned first of all about ourselves, our jobs, our standard of living, our safety, our finances, our health, our children, and other people's opinions of us.

Our fears render us more passive; we are more of a spectator and less of an actor.

Social media contributes to this increasing obsession we are developing about ourselves and about how others see us.

The cult of the emoticon on social media makes us more sensitive to the way others react to what we say and what we post. We want to be loved; we want to be accepted, but strangely, absurdly, we do everything to isolate ourselves.

We know how to look at our mobile phones but we do not know how to dialogue, nor are we very interested in it. We have become narcissists.

We are emotionally fragile, less inclined to tolerate views that are not ours, quicker to claim offense, quicker to judge, less inclined to forgive.

As a result, we become ghetto oriented. We crave for the fellowship of the clan or the tribe, where we know our opinions are accepted, welcomed, even lauded, but we withdraw from a world that easily offends our increasingly emotionally fragile psyche.

Outside of our safe places, we are silent. We do not debate and do not welcome debate as we are fearful of judgement, of differing views and of moral and intellectual challenges.

It is time to sound the alarm, to stop being fearful and to become more responsible.

This book is largely about the threats to our freedom, threats from opinions and expressions of thought which are compounded by a chronic passive indifference among the majority of the Australian population.

It is also about the dumbing down of our intellect through the emotional and intellectual manipulation of the media, the elites and the political parties.

It is about what happens, not just to the individual but to society as a whole, when a significant number of persons are not heard or fear being heard in the marketplace of opinions and ideas.

It is about the ongoing devaluation of our national intellectual capital and of the intellectual capital of the Western world.

We no longer think; we just feel. We are dumbing down intellectually but also emotionally. As Thomas Sowell once said: *"the problem isn't that Johnny can't read. The problem isn't even that Johnny can't think. The problem is that Johnny doesn't know what thinking is; he confuses it with feeling."*

We act on the basis of impulses and emotions, grounded in a 'new morality' which is no morality at all. We are not even consistent in what we do or say. The new 'woke' philosophy which we are asked to endorse is full of contradictions.

To whom shall we turn, might you well ask?

Already, in 2014, Emeritus Professor Frank Furedi raised the question in his book *"Where have all the intellectuals gone?"*[i]

He raised the question because already, at that time, he could pinpoint how academic freedom was denied at university, how ideology was trumping any notion of what is true and factual and how the respect for Knowledge had already been lost.

He also remarked that our society was becoming increasingly technologically savvy and that knowledge was becoming more specialised, resulting in '*intellectuals (being) discouraged from looking at the big picture ... (with) discussions ... increasingly self-referential and not designed to communicate and engage people outside a specific field of speciality.'*

It is fair to say that the trend towards a more utilitarian type of education has been gathering momentum for decades, so in the main, at primary and secondary school levels, the aim has been to prepare students for the workplace, for a vocation or job, rather than teaching them how to think broadly or to perceive the bigger picture.

Teacher shortage also compounds this problem. It would appear that a number of universities in Australia lower entry standards for teaching degrees to cash in on fees; this makes it difficult for many less talented students to cope with the complexity of the courses they are enrolled in and, this in turn, has disastrous consequences on the quality of the education delivered in our schools.[2]

In addition, curricula are now being changed to promote the so-called ideology of 'diversity' which is not diversity at all but a particular type of neo-cultural Marxism. For instance, the Australian curriculum at both primary and secondary levels is continually being restructured to give greater priority to ideology rather than to history, which in turn paves the way for the university to take this even further, to a new level, with the ultimate aim of taking this woke ideology into the workplace and promoting it as the new ethos of our institutions, business organisations and the like.

Alarmingly, original intellectual thought is no longer encouraged. Rather, independent thinking is now subservient to ideology, and facts are allowed to be misrepresented; reporting must be edited to fit in with the promotion of the current brand

---

[2] The Federal Minister of Education was recently reported in the media as saying that only 50 per cent of students graduate from a teaching degree (The Week End Australian, 20-21 August 2022)

of postmodern woke philosophy. Any academic courageous enough to oppose this may lose his university tenure – for instance, James Cook University's Peter Ridd who dared to argue that the Great Barrier Reef was not an ecological disaster.

Freedom of expression is the most important issue facing the planet.

What can we do about this? What strategy should we deploy?

At the outset, we should acknowledge that if we do not value our freedom of thought and expression, if we do not practice it, then we are likely to lose it.

Freedoms are not inalienable rights; freedoms need to be cherished and claimed and re-claimed to be preserved.

The basic weapon in the fight for freedom of expression is the practice of it.

The richness of a society and the sustainability of a particular civilisation is not to be measured mainly, if not exclusively as some would have it, by the range of emotions that are permissible to express but also by the thoughts raised by its public intellectuals and by the type of debates that are allowed in the nation's 'marketplace'.

Freedom of thought and expression is the absolute number one priority in the world today.

It outranks everything else, ranging from climate change, Third World issues, abortion, euthanasia, crime, slavery, etc. Not that any of these issues are unimportant, but rather because *to be able to debate them properly, to hear opposite, dissonant views, one must first of all preserve not only the right to one's opinion but also the right to a respectful public hearing.*

Our thoughts define who we are and one of the founding fathers of epistemology, the Frenchman René Descartes, already declared in the 17th century "Cogito, ergo sum" (I think, therefore I am).

Unfortunately, nowadays sound thinking is no longer

encouraged; rather we are told to live according to our emotions. "If it feels good to you, do it," is the new behavioural benchmark. This is an irresponsible, infantile philosophy that we cannot live or teach consistently. What parent, for instance, would say to her child that if she thinks it feels good to attack her sister, she should do it?

Emotions are important, but thinking should come first. Emotions do not arise in a vacuum; they should be the product of our thoughts and beliefs. Progress is not achieved by focusing first of all on changing our emotions but rather on changing our thoughts. The thought should dictate what the emotion should be.

Reasoning should come first, but it does not. Jonathan Haidt in his book [ii]*The Righteous Mind, why good people are divided by politics and religion,* explains how intuitive thoughts come first, reasoning second. He uses the metaphor of a rider on an elephant. The rider (reasoning) should be in charge, but unfortunately the elephant (intuitions) takes the lead and the rider becomes the servant of the elephant.

If intuitions, feelings and passions were always good, this should present no problem, but unfortunately, a quick look at history or even a time of private self-introspection will reveal that this is not often the case.

We are now living in an era where original thinking is no longer welcomed and where we are expected to feel a certain way. Certainly, we are allowed to think but only in a particular way, provided we have an acceptable view of history, a politically correct view of what is right and wrong, in turn anchored into the type of emotions the elites want us to express.

Whilst the new 'elites' are telling us what is right and wrong, they are actually designing a new morality and they have infiltrated the key spheres of influence: the media, the courts and the institutions of learning.

An audit conducted by the Institute of Public Affairs in 2020 found that 'themes of class, race and gender dominate history, literature, politics and social studies courses at the expense of traditional disciplinary content' in Bachelor of Arts subjects offered in ten Australian universities[iii].

Rapidly, our population and the populations of most countries in the Western World are being indoctrinated into a particular mindset. The power of social media in this regard is indisputable. For instance, it is a well-known fact that Facebook bans people from posting opinions that are considered offensive in the judgement of its administrators. The so-called *offenders* will be blocked from publishing further posts for a period of time (and sometimes even permanently) should they fail to desist.

What is less known, however, is how the Internet (Google) provides us with biased research results.

In his book *The Madness of Crowds,* Britain-based Douglas Murray explains how this 'selection bias' operates:

> *If you tell Google that you would like to see the images of "black men", the images that come up are all portrait photos of black men ... By contrast, a search for "White men" first throws up an image of David Beckham – who is white – but then the second is of a black model. From there, every line of five images has either one or two black men in the line-up. Many of the images of white men are of people convicted of crimes with taglines such as 'Beware of the average white man" and "White men are bad."[iv]*

One might find it bizarre, if not contradictory, that in a postmodern world where objective Truth is deemed to be unattainable, we are being brainwashed into adopting a particular code of ethics, a particular mindset as if any other philosophy or thought patterns were utterly immoral or untrue.

How did we get to this point, and can anything be done to reverse our trajectory into intellectual and moral oblivion? If not, what will the consequences be on the lives of ordinary Australians? On the quality of our relationships? On what blends us, unites us as a nation? On our freedom of worship? On democracy, as such? May we shield ourselves from a path that has been embarked upon, not solely by Australia but by most Western nations?

What is our core problem, the cause of our loss of freedom of expression and thought?

Our core problem is simply this:

Our Australian society, but more particularly our future leaders, our university scholars, our researchers, are being taught by the new 'elites' (aka the new Left) that a perpetual conflict exists between two types of individuals: the oppressor and the oppressed.

Worst still, that all of us fall into one or the other category through random circumstances dictated by our cultural heritage; and furthermore, we are also told that our assigned category is in the nature of a life-long label that is unchangeable.

The current brand of philosophy we are plagued with asserts that anyone who is white, born in a Western world country, heterosexual, well-educated and middle-class belongs categorically to the camp of the oppressor. On the other hand, a poor person, particularly a black or lesbian or transexual, is automatically placed on the side of the oppressed.

The oppressors are heavily criticised for the so-called crimes of oppression they commit. They are accused of being racist but considered incapable of being sympathetic to the other side. Their assigned identity is a lifelong one.

This explains why university academic, Robin di Angelo, can write:

Being good or bad is not relevant. Racism is a multilayered system embedded in our culture. All of us are socialized into the system of racism. Racism cannot be avoided. Whites have blind spots on racism, and I have blind spots on racism. Racism is complex, and I don't have to understand every nuance of the feedback to validate that feedback. Whites are/I am unconsciously invested in racism. Bias is implicit and unconscious.[v]

It follows, therefore, that the oppressed identities cannot ever win because the oppressors are unable to cease being oppressors.

In other words, cultural norms define who we are.

To the average Australian, all this sounds like utter nonsense, and that is, of course, because it is exactly that.

Unfortunately, the 'elites' of the New Left think this is serious; they are very vocal about it.

Consequently, a very significant amount of brainwashing is currently taking place in our schools and universities in order to ensure that the new generations take hold of that view and uphold and nurture the belief in a society perpetually in conflict at all levels.

To achieve this, history is being rewritten, and as the expression goes nowadays, **we cancel culture**.

We now teach that a factual balanced view of history is deemed to be unattainable because our language (discourse) is always going to be the fruit of our own cultural prejudices. Objective truth cannot be attained, and history is rewritten to serve one's philosophical views. Events that were considered to be indisputable renditions of the truth in years past are now narrated differently and quoted as examples of a society dominated by some at the expense of others.

For instance, although much has already been said about the

'stolen generation' and whilst the facts indubitably testify about the horrors and injustices endured by the Aboriginal population, it is no longer appropriate to teach that the so-called European oppressors built schools, hospitals and entire townships and that they contributed abundantly to the richness modern Australia currently enjoys culturally, intellectually and economically.

Such new opinions, such profound cultural upheavals, have not occurred by chance. Rather, they are the result of a journey started long ago on a very philosophical slippery slope that placed Mankind at the centre of the universe: humanism.

The loss of faith in a redeeming God gave us the existentialist movement (Alfred Camus and others) and the existentialist theory of the absurd. The life-has-no-meaning movement. The nihilism and despair that resulted from it in turn gave rise to the early French postmodernists (Foucault, Derrida, Lyotard) who tried to resurrect the Left from the failures of economic Marxism.

Gradually, this led us to a place where both God and Man were removed from the debate; all that counts now is your immovable identity and on which side of the conflict you have been positioned by indomitable cultural forces.

The purpose of this book is to explore the causes of this past historical trajectory in more detail and suggest a manifesto for remedial action.

As stated earlier, this book is likely to be controversial. If it is, in some way, then my purpose has been fulfilled. I want to encourage debate and discussion. I am prepared to review my opinions, refine my arguments because without debate, without discussion, we are bound to perish culturally, intellectually and spiritually. Without debate, without freedom of expression, society is doomed; civilisation perishes.

Summary

We are living in a culture of isolation, created out of fear of the reactions to what we say or write from those who do not agree with us. This is already starting to have significant repercussions on the future of intellectual thought, democracy and religious life.

An expanding woke culture is acknowledging only two types of individuals: oppressors and oppressed; anything belonging to past or present Western culture is deemed to be oppressive and needs to be "cancelled".

History is being rewritten to highlight only the evils committed by Western Europeans and we seem to be unable to provide an objective, balanced view of history. Emotions now dictate how we think and we are increasingly indoctrinated into a new mentality by the current 'elites'.

We are silenced unless we agree, we are becoming fearful of voicing our thoughts and are increasingly sensitive and fragile to what others say or think of us. Out of fear of no longer being accepted, we are silenced. In fact, we self-censor.

This results in a loss of the most important asset any society may have: freedom of expression.

We seem to be oblivious to it.

I am writing this book to sound the alarm and to stress that without freedom of expression, there can be no democracy, no intellectual advance and no spiritual life.

Loss of freedom of expression is the death knell of civilised society.

Chapter 1

The Death of Human Dignity

"Dignity is as essential to human life as water, food and oxygen."

(Laura Hillenbrand)

We hear much today about "diversity", but not so much about human dignity. The implication seems to be that by respecting diversity, we uphold human dignity.

Indeed, current postmodern thinking teaches that we can only respect one another or recognise each other's human dignity if we accept the fact that we all have diverse identities.

However, these diverse identities are not simply different personality types, they are group identities.

What matters is the group, not the individual. Hence there is really no individual human dignity any longer, there is only group dignity.

Postmodernism does not assign value to the individual, to the human; it only assigns value to diverse identities. Dignity is only assigned to the group, not to the individual.

> *"... to postmodern theorists, the notion of the autonomous individual is largely a myth. The individual, like everything else, is a product of powerful discourses and culturally constructed knowledge ... The postmodern view ... rejects the individual... and instead focuses on*

small, local groups as the producers of knowledge, values, and discourses…. It focuses on sets of people who are understood to be positioned in the same way - by race, sex or class, for example- and have the same experiences and perceptions due to this positioning."[vi]

We are only identified by the group we belong to. For instance, we could be either black, white, cisgender, gay, poor, racist, disabled or fat. These groups determine how we can be identified as a person. The racist, white and cisgender are considered to be bad or immoral because they are seen as oppressor identities. On the other hand, the black, gay, poor, disabled and fat are good or moral because they are seen as oppressed identities.

Consequently, the individual does not count anymore. The group, the class, the faction only does. Without belonging to the group, the individual has no more value than animals or plants. This is how we can now justify abortion, infanticide and euthanasia.

As shocking as this might sound to the average reader, this philosophy is only a logical progression for a world that only believes that matter exists. A world that claims we are the product of random chance and time. We are told that we are only an accumulation of molecules, matter, cells; there is no soul, there is no supernatural power, there is no God; or so the postmodern philosophers would have us believe.

We no longer find our identity in a Creator God, a true Personal Being, who made us in His image, we no longer derive our worth from being the creatures of the Divinity; instead, we find our value in experiential living.

We now live for the experience, for the thrill, for the kicks, for the pleasure, for the accolade.

Our true identity is where we find our pleasure, our

happiness. We, therefore, look for the experience to be a tool to discovering our true identity.

For instance, a young person looking for experience might find more pleasure in a different identity than what she was assigned to at birth, she is female, but the experience of being a male gives her greater pleasure, so she thinks her true identity is to become transgender. The transgender status is now what she perceives to be her source of value and dignity. Remove, however, that identity from her and she believes she is nothing again.

This is a philosophy of despair, a philosophy of no hope. We no longer have any human dignity, any value; we only carry the value that is ascribed to our group.

The group defines our identity, and we are prisoners of the group we belong to.

We are therefore encouraged to suppress our thoughts, our words, and instead adopt the thoughts, words and actions of the group. The peer pressure is enormous; we are taught we will find security, meaning, support and dignity in the group, not in our ourselves, as individuals. We are not speaking in our name anymore; we now speak in the name of the group, be it the black, the white, the disabled, the fat, the refugee, the homosexual, the lesbian, the transgender or any other group.

It is as if the group has some spiritual value, whilst the individual is only matter, molecule.

The group is 'upstairs', the individual 'downstairs'. To find meaning, the individual must climb 'upstairs' and, once there, open the 'right' room to find where his true identity lies.

Too bad if it takes years to find the strength to get out of the closet, to climb upstairs and to find out exactly which door to open to find the right group we belong to; until this is done, we are told we have no value and therefore no dignity.

How did we get from a position where Man was the measure

of all things, the meaning of all things, hence from a humanist vantage point to a position where Man is now nothing and the group is everything?

The answer to this question starts by recognising that humanism was never going to be the solution because Man is not everything and does not have the answer to everything.

The answer to everything is God.

However, nowadays, many refuse to accept God and therefore stumble to find meaning.

Many now look elsewhere for an answer and the postmodern now puts up his hand and replies that the answer to the meaning of life is group identity.

The strange thing is that although postmodernism claims that our identity is a cultural construct and therefore imposed by our circumstances and upbringing; it also claims that one has to have the freedom to choose one's identity and that it is precisely that freedom of choice that gives us dignity.

The contradiction in this statement is self-evident and illustrates the lack of logic of postmodernism, something I will discuss further on in this chapter and which reflects the fact that this philosophy is based on emotivism, not on logic.

At this stage, let me merely point out the frightening consequences of believing that dignity can only be preserved as long as freedom of choice exists.

Indeed, if we passionately believe that our ability to make choices is what gives us dignity, we can only conclude that anyone deprived of cognitive capacity has no human dignity, that the young baby has no dignity and that the prisoner in a concentration camp has no human dignity. Few people (with the notable exception of Peter Singer) would believe this, but this is, unfortunately, the logical conclusion of postmodern philosophy if it is applied consistently to our living environment.[vii]

Furthermore, if society is going to allow people to make

unrestricted choices in order, allegedly, to protect their human dignity, we are either assuming that human dignity is upheld because all choices are good or else, we believe that human dignity has nothing to do with good or bad choices but only with the <u>freedom</u> to make such choices.

Suddenly, we have no right to say to someone that their choice is good or bad, that they are taking unreasonable risks.

If my child's dignity depends on his or her ability to make choices, I have no right anymore to prevent him or her to touch a hot stove.

The consequences are tragic: good only exists if one can make any decisions one wishes to make; external judgement is not tolerated; hence anarchy prevails. There is no arbiter, no Supreme Judge, no benchmark. Religion (particularly Christianity which teaches that all human beings are tainted in various degrees by evil and need salvation by a totally holy and just God), has no place; debate has no place.

Voicing a different opinion is deemed to be offensive because it implies that I should not believe or act in a particular way.

A philosophy of contradictions.

Nowadays, being nonjudgmental is applauded as a core moral quality. The idea is that one is entitled to behave as one wants provided that no criticism is levied at the other.

As a result, we are creating borders, divisions where we say that you can only enter my territory, my space, on my own terms. Indeed, do not come across on your own terms, with your beliefs and prejudices, come across to me without judgment, without opinions that might make me feel uncomfortable.

If you are not prepared to do that, stay on your side of the border; do not reach out to me.

If you do not agree with me, you are bad because you are

unlike me, and I am good.

Since postmodernist woke philosophy classifies people either as 'good' or 'bad', with no mixture of both epithets, it follows that we are either nonracist black or racist white, and neither are capable of crossing 'the border' to reach out to that other side, because both are conditioned to bear the label society has assigned them through cultural norms.

We are therefore condemned to sociological isolation, imprisoned inside our prejudices and cultural borders. Silent, fragile and isolated.

Yet, the same woke elites who preach the inevitability of sociological isolation will support the abolition of geographical borders.

Strong impassable sociological borders but no geographical borders. Nonracist black and racist white cannot ever live in harmony, and yet Europe, Australia, the Western World are meant to drop all geographical borders and accept an increasing number of arrivals of non-Westerners who claim asylum, refugee status.

At least, this was the position until recently, just prior to the COVID international pandemic.

Modern Europe does indeed illustrate the point well.

It is a well-known fact that there is no need for entry visas or the like to move freely from one European country to another in a pre-COVID world. The European Union is borderless to all its members and yet how many refuse to integrate and instead erect their own sociological borders, their ghettos where white Europeans are not welcome?

Also, it is not just countries that have become borderless but all manner of groups and associations.

In the words of Frank Furedi:

> *"Just Google the words "without borders" – what you*

will find is not just Médecins sans Frontières (Doctors without borders) but a bewildering array of organisations that aspire to achieve the highly acclaimed status of being without borders. Engineers, musicians, chemists, veterinarians, executives, librarians, builders, plumbers, lawyers, astronomers, creatives, journalists, rabbis, herbalists, women, sex workers, acupuncturists, clowns. [viii]

There is also the whole problem of intersectionality.

Intersectionality attempts to deal with multiple identities that an individual might possess and the conflicts that arise between these identities.

Keeping such identities within their own 'borders' becomes immensely difficult. For instance, how do you reconcile a gay (oppressed) identity with a highly educated white (oppressor) identity? How can you manage not being conflicted if you are gay and white?

The truth is that this woke postmodern philosophy, which is rapidly gaining momentum, is a philosophy of contradictions, a reaffirmation of the philosophy of the Absurd developed by the early 20th-century existential school of thought.

This philosophy preaches against intolerance but, at the same time, is intolerant of the intolerant. It is repressive, oppressive, dictatorial, and, although it claims that it upholds dignity and human rights, it uses the tools of coercion, brainwashing and dictatorship to achieve its ends.

It uses means that its ends do not support.

For instance, it fights for freedom but, at the same time, it is not shy of imposing restrictions on thought, expression and belief.

It claims to support human dignity by upholding diversity, but it is actually demeaning and humiliating.

It also shows a lack of emotional intelligence.

Take, for instance, the issue of euthanasia.

Proponents of euthanasia seek to justify their position by saying that they wish to preserve human dignity.

They show great emotional turmoil at the thought that some might die in great pain, and they ask what dignity is there in allowing people to die in circumstances when we would not allow a dog to live? Yet, they lack the emotional intelligence to ask the follow-up question: What dignity is there in death? – particularly if death is the end of everything, if there is nothing beyond the tomb or the ashes, apart from some romantic idea of the spirit of the departed watching over us?

They seem to lack the emotional intelligence to ask why we allow euthanasia to take place in cases of chronic pain for the terminally ill with less than six months to live. Why not kill everyone in chronic pain, whether terminally ill or not? Why six months? Why only allow those who can express their wishes clearly to show the exit option? What about the mentally deficient, the young child etc?

If you google 'emotional intelligence', you may read that emotional intelligence has the following attributes:

1. *"Self-management – You're able to control impulsive feelings and behaviours, manage your emotions in healthy ways, take initiative, follow through on commitments, and adapt to changing circumstances.*

2. *Self-awareness – You recognise your own emotions and how they affect your thoughts and behaviour. You know your strengths and weaknesses and have self-confidence.*

3. *Social awareness – You have empathy. You can understand the emotions, needs, and concerns of other people, pick up on emotional cues, feel comfortable*

socially, and recognise the power dynamics in a group
or organisation.

4. *Relationship management – You know how to develop*
   and maintain good relationships, communicate clearly,
   inspire and influence others, work well in a team, and
   manage conflict[ix] "

Woke philosophy is deficient on each of these counts.

It fails on self-management as it cannot control impulsive feelings and behaviours which categorise people on the basis of the colour of their skin. White is bad, black is good. Black lives matter; white lives matter less, if at all.

It fails on self-awareness as it does not realise that the outrage it expresses in condemning all aspects of Western thought and civilisation is actually an expression of the racist nature this same woke philosophy claims to oppose.

It fails on social awareness as it fails to have empathy towards those who fall outside the particular identities approved by the woke elites.

It fails on relationship management as it perpetuates the very class conflict it claims to oppose.

So why is it gathering such momentum? Why is it so popular?

The answer is largely because of the power held by the spheres of influence who promote this philosophy.

These spheres of influence are the media, the universities, and the legislative and executive arms of government.

We shall examine in another chapter how this influence is exercised in different ways by each of these spheres, but we should acknowledge at the outset that their joint success is largely based on the promotion of a new moral code.

Summary

Human rights are now being displaced by group rights.

It seems that what it means to be human is to acquire a group identity, preferably an oppressed identity. Acceptance of an increasing panoply of diverse identities is the new prerequisite to respect and dignity of the other.

The group is now the custodian of dignity, hence the pressure to belonging to one and of endorsing the values and the language of the group. Good and evil now reside in the groups to which we belong; the oppressed identities are moral and the oppressor identities are immoral.

Anything not vested into one of the oppressed identities (gay, black, disabled, fat etc) may no longer be tolerated by the new morality.

Woke postmodernism, therefore, uses means that its ends do not support. It fights for freedom, but at the same time, it is not shy of imposing restrictions on thought, expression and belief. It claims to support human dignity by upholding diversity, but it is actually demeaning and humiliating. It also shows a lack of emotional intelligence.

The woke movement fails in emotional control management, social awareness and relationship management and is only gathering momentum thanks to the coordinated efforts of the spheres of influence, vested in the media, the educational sector, the justice system and our governments. This book will attempt to suggest some solutions to counteract this significant threat to the basic freedoms of our society.

Chapter 2

Culture and Morality

"If the state of nature is the ideal, and if society corrupts, then the history of society becomes the history of the corruption and oppression of human nature"

(Carl Trueman in his exposition of Rousseau's philosophy)

A society's convictions about what is proper to believe define that society's specific culture.

As most of what we used to believe or do is now being challenged by a significant minority, we who live in Australia and most of the Western world find ourselves in the midst of a cultural moral revolution.

We often hear the phrase "cancel culture", but, of course, culture cannot disappear because countries, groups, individual persons will always have some customs and beliefs.

So, the expression "cancel culture" is misleading because it conveys the impression that anything that is cultural is bad.

Yet, the proponents of the "cancel culture" movement are not promoting the absence of any customs or beliefs but rather the type of culture that the Western World has acquired.

The woke movement is against anything the Western World has accomplished; it would dispute that our understanding of culture is moral. When, as the Oxford Dictionary defines it, we say that a person is cultured because he or she has refined taste, good manners and good education, the woke movement accuses us of racism. By this, it means that we discriminate in favour of those who are privileged and place a lesser value on those who are not; we discriminate against those who have not been brought up to be polite and well-schooled.

Consequently, the accomplishments of well-known personalities, Churchill, Beethoven, Captain Cook, the kings and queens of England, Rodin, Victor Hugo, Shakespeare, Newton, anyone whose name and contribution to society has been preserved by history is to be subjected to ridicule or outright condemnation, on the grounds of racism, misogyny or any of the other popular facile denunciations. The achievements of any of these people need to be suppressed and consigned to permanent oblivion in the collective mindset of all present and future generations. Museums, art galleries should be closed down, statues torn down and books burnt. These are privileged people; they deserve condemnation; they have "colonised" our current way of thinking with their ideas and prejudices, with their unacceptable set of values.

The judicial system appears to have no immunity against this devastating trend: in 2021, four protesters were acquitted by a jury in Bristol for vandalising the statue of 17th-century slave trader, Edward Colston, rolling it through the street and dumping it in the harbour.[xi]

Respected sociologist Frank Furedi remarked that the Welsh National Opera was planning to run a series of lectures on Madame Butterfly to highlight the issues of "imperialism and colonialism"[xii]. He also alerts us to a recent Gender and Equity Diversity forum held under the auspices of the Australian Music Centre where the idea that "quality comes first was dismissed on the grounds that it ignores the inherent privileges that many are afforded."

Furthermore, government budgetary allocation is now

trending away from funding the preservation of our archives. Since 2015, the National Archives of Australia has suffered an annual appropriation decrease of nearly $9M and has shed approximately a fifth of its staff.[xiii]

The woke elite wants a *tabula rasa*, a clean slate on which to build their new ideology, their new "morality".

It is absolutely frightening for one might well ask what edifice would these elites wish to erect on a cultural *terra nullius*?

The woke elites naturally believe a better new society can only be erected if the present one is totally eradicated, and to that extent, much of their thinking derives from the philosophical work of the eighteenth-century French philosopher Jean-Jacques Rousseau.

Rousseau believed that civilisation was bad. He thought it led to degenerative and immoral practices. Well before the dawn of our culture of materialism, Rousseau had understood that riches and material well-being (which are the product of so-called "civilisation") make mankind more dissatisfied (always wanting more), more envious, more selfish and more cruel.

Civilisation, therefore, gives birth to inequality, a world of "haves" and "haves not", and the 1789 French Revolution (which Rousseau did not live long enough to witness) was pretty much the culmination of his thinking, at least in the mind of the key French revolutionary leaders of the times, such as Terror leader movement, Robespierre.

Although in the manner of Rousseau, the woke movement condemns our civilisation and dreams of a utopian new world, the present elites do not seem to realise that what they evoke is another form of inequality and division where those who do not subscribe to the new ethos would be forced to lose their freedom of thought and expression and be very much treated as second-class citizens.

An oppressive, totalitarian alternative where the new *moral* groups, aka the less educated, the more fringe elements of our society would have the upper ground, to compensate for the centuries during which they supposedly suffered a lack of social and intellectual recognition from the Western elites.

In fact, this is exactly what happened during Mao's ironically named 'Great Leap Forward' and during Stalin's Reign of Terror. True intellectuals were condemned to imprisonment, exile to remote areas, or death, while faithful party apparatchiks and manipulators gained great wealth and power.

History repeats itself, unbeknown to many of the younger generations.

Naturally, one of the key targets is Christianity. Christian missionaries are key culprits. They are accused of imposing on other cultures a set of values and beliefs that has "colonised" the understanding and lifestyles of those non-Western cultures. This is the school of thought of the New Left that believes that Australia was invaded and that we had no right to impose our way of life on the Aboriginal population of this country. This is the school of thought that will quite rightly scream at the horrors perpetrated upon the "stolen generation", the abuse and molestation of children by some segments of the Christian church, but it is also the school of thought that will claim that building hospitals, schools, roads and housing was evil, that it was culture rape and that any type of colonisation in the past has been evil.

Interestingly, this is also the school of thought that overlooks the dark side of the indigenous culture, especially where women are concerned, with the disturbing level of past and present domestic violence in remote communities.

Yes, there has been a significant number of horrors, hatred and evil perpetrated in Western culture, but a little balance would not go astray. Ignoring the achievements of the past and starting from nothing hardly seems to be an ideal way to rebuild a fairer, more equitable, more compassionate society, assuming, of course, that this is still the goal of the woke movement.

When all has been said, however, we discover that the fundamental issue is not the 'culture wars' as they have been labelled, but rather the emergence of a new morality which has nothing to do with the old. As a matter of fact, the new morality accuses the old to be immoral.

What we used to consider "moral" is now immoral, and this is why the New Left now considers that its achievements reflect a progression towards a more moral society.

The yardstick used to measure this progress is different from the old.

In the past, morality in most Western European countries was measured by adherence to the teachings of the Christian church, derived in turn from the teachings of the Bible. There was some common understanding of what these teachings meant.

For instance, everybody knew what was meant by the commandment "Love thy neighbour like thyself".

Everyone understood that loving your neighbour like yourself meant self-sacrifice, parting with things I could do or keep in order for my neighbour to enjoy them or possess them. In contrast, selfish love, which is idolatry, has always been condemned in the Bible account. We are not meant to love to get something in return, but we are meant to love without counting the cost or expecting a return.

The issue nowadays is that when people talk about loving others, they mean something entirely different. They mean leaving them alone to do what they want. In that sort of love, I do not need to sacrifice anything I own or possess; I simply need to let people be, irrespective of the consequences they might suffer.

So, if a young person, still lacking maturity and discernment, decides to take on a different gender than the one assigned at birth, the new morality prevents me from discouraging that person who, unfortunately, might be totally unaware of the risks he or she takes.

Case stories citing regret among transgender people and a desire "to return" are brushed away as anecdotal and somewhat irrelevant. In any case, we are told this is their problem, not yours. Just leave them alone.

An interesting case in this regard is that of Keira Bell who went all the way to the British High Court.[xiv]. The case concerns the legal requirements of obtaining consent to carry out medical treatment in treating children with gender dysphoria. The court heard that for the year 2019/2020, 161 children were prescribed puberty-suppressing drugs by the Gender Identity Development Service, run by the Tavistock & Portman NHS Trust. The court was told that the age profile of these children was as follows:

- 3 were 10 or 11 years old at the time of referral;
- 13 were 12 years old;
- 10 were 13 years old;
- 24 were 14 years old;
- 45 were 15 years old;
- 51 were 16 years old;
- 15 were 17 or 18 years old.

As common sense would expect, the court considered that it was highly unlikely that a child under 13 would be competent to give consent to the administration of puberty blockers and that "it was also doubtful that a child aged 14 or 15 could understand or weigh the long-term risks and consequences of the administration of puberty-blocking drugs".

However, this has not stopped the transgender movement in its tracks, and the initial victory for Keira Bell who wanted to detransition back to her birth biological gender was later on overturned on appeal by the British courts. [3]

In fact, some jurisdictions have now passed legislation preventing offering any advice that might deter anyone from transitioning or de-transitioning.

This state of affairs applies to all: not only to young children who lack the capacity to make informed decisions but to older vulnerable individuals who suffer from the same handicap. The State does not interfere and does not want anyone to interfere.

How is this supposed to uphold human dignity?

A case in point is that of Nathan Verhelst who died in Belgium in 2013[xv]. Nathan was born a girl and, following years of acute rejection, decided in her late thirties to transgender as a male. After three major sex-change operations, she looked into the mirror and was disgusted by the results: her breasts and penis did not match her expectations, and depression soon followed. A few years later, at the age of 44, only a year after the last sex change procedure, she applied to the Belgian authorities to be euthanised.

Supporters of the transgender movement and, more generally, the woke movement, will undoubtedly justify this horrific outcome by saying that Nathan was given the freedom to exercise a choice and that his human dignity was upheld by virtue of that freedom. No thought, however, will be given to the fact, that maybe – just maybe – this man/woman was vulnerable, conflicted, confused and unable to make a valid decision.

How loving therefore was it to leave him to take another gender than the one assigned at his birth? How much advice did

---

[3] Since then, the British authorities ordered the closing down of the Tavistock Clinic following concerns raised by doctors that young patients were being referred to a gender transitioning path too quickly. The UK's National Health Service also released some new multi-disciplinary team guidelines for the treatment of gender dysphoria

he really receive before he embarked on this life changing series of surgical interventions? Did the Belgian government uphold his human dignity by allowing him to degrade himself physically and psychologically to the point where he no longer wanted to live?

Unfortunately, as mentioned earlier, the woke movement has no time for individual human dignity; woke philosophy attributes dignity only to the group, the identity clan, not the individual person.

By allowing Nancy to transgender to a man, the rights of the transgender group were upheld, but the dignity of Nancy/Nathan was trodden upon.

Furthermore, this is not an isolated case. More recently, in Australia, Ollie Davies initially transgendered from man to woman but only to revert, later, back to being a man. He now has a wife but cannot conceive anymore. He has been reported in the media for saying:

> '*I think there is a massive population of people who actually don't have gender dysphoria who are now either being pushed toward or themselves being drawn forward the tender affirmative care pathway. It has infiltrated the culture, it comes from doctors, it comes from the media, it comes from social media, it comes from the peak LGBTQI+ organisations and the marketing that they put out, it's everywhere telling you if you don't feel like you fit the stereotype, you might be trans. For me, it felt like I'd pretty much been involved in a cult.*'[xvi]

In an article authored by Bernard Lane and published recently in the online magazine *Quillette*[xvii], we are informed that in "a Canadian primary school, a six-year-old girl was reportedly upset and puzzled after her teacher showed the class a YouTube video titled *He, She and They?!? Gender, Queer Kid Stuff #2.*" The video stated that some people aren't boys and girls; (then) another day, the teacher asked the children to place themselves on a gender-spectrum diagram. The six-year-old put herself at the "girl" end of the spectrum, only to be told by the teacher that "girls are not real and boys are not real."

We are indeed dealing with a new morality, and the problem is that the elites perceive it to be a better one.

One of the key tenets of this new morality is the absence of parental rights. It is no longer "moral" for parents to be the ultimate authority on how they wish their children to be educated. In this new world, parents cannot be trusted; they are ignorant or narrow-minded. Hence, the ultimate authority, the ultimate moral judgement, is made by the State or by State institutions or private institutions recognised by the State to be acting in the interest of the public at large.

This explains why the federal government-hosted Student Wellbeing Hub can publish online the following material. [xviii]

> *"The person who understands most about their gender affirmation or transition is the student themselves (sic)... consideration should be given to the age and maturity of the student and whether it would be appropriate to involve the student's parent(s)? or guardian(s) in each decision... it may be possible to consider a student a mature minor and able to make decisions without parental consent."*

Summary

Postmodern woke philosophy does not advocate a substitute morality that one might have the option to endorse or to reject; indeed, it does not provide an "elective" morality but insists, instead, on a compulsive new world order.

It demands we make a "tabula rasa", a clean slate of anything achieved by Western civilisation in the past.

Whilst wokeism denounces quite appropriately all of the horrors perpetrated by European missionaries and men of power in the past, it does not provide a balanced view of history and is simply intent on burning the books of the past.

The cancel culture movement takes no prisoners to its cause and brandishes a new notion of "love", anchored in the "live and let be" slogan.

As such, woke activists believe that nobody has the right to interfere in another person's life (with the notable exception of themselves).

This means that actions that are clearly dangerous to an individual are not challenged even though they might result in psychological trauma, mental illness or even, as in the case of Nathan Verhelst, death.

Chapter 3

The Seeds of the Present Catastrophe

How did we get here?

How did we get to a situation where human rights no longer exist and where humans are captive to their own individual cultural background over which they have no influence?

How did we get to a situation where you are either totally good and therefore a victim or totally bad and therefore a bully, with nothing in the middle?

At first glance, such a narrow-minded view of humanity appears absurd.

However, in some ways, it is not difficult to demonstrate that throughout the ages, society always had its oppressors and its oppressed.

The Old Testament Bible, which records historical events that are four and a half thousand years old, is largely the story of how the Jews were oppressed in captivity, initially by the Egyptians and later on by the Assyrians and Babylonians.

Outside the Bible, in some of the earliest records, such as, for example, the Code of Hammurabi (c.1760 BC), slavery is treated as an established institution and death is prescribed for anyone who helps a slave to escape or who shelters a fugitive.

In the Middle Ages and until the advent of the Magna Carta, the king's rule over the nobles was absolute and in turn the nobles' rule over the general populace (the serfs) was likewise unopposable.

The French Revolution of 1789 illustrates the revolt of the Third Estate (the general populace) against the tyranny of the king and the privileges and wealth of the Catholic Church.

Karl Marx would not have reached his level of notoriety had there not been some serious exploitation of the working classes by the owners of capital.

One could go on.

Nevertheless, to view all of history from the perspective of irremediable and perpetual conflict is negative, unhelpful and biased. It is also very damaging.

It is particularly damaging because the postmodernist elites believe that the more educated, so-called privileged classes are no longer entitled to access a public audience. They have had their "say", so to speak, and they are overrepresented in the marketplace of ideas and debate. Their accessibility to language and education gives them too much power in contrast to the non-white races. These so-called privileged white, educated, Christian heterosexuals have far too long used language and speech as a power tool to subjugate those of a different cultural background, who are now arbitrarily grouped under the label of "oppressed".

How did we get to think this way?

Stephen Hicks, in his book *Explaining Postmodernism*, [xix] provides a sound and detailed answer to this question.

Starting with the Enlightenment era, he explains how that movement "*developed those features of the modern world that many now take largely for granted: liberal politics and free markets, scientific progress and technological innovation ... all (depending) upon confidence on the power of reason.*"[xx]

He then goes on to explain how by the middle of the eighteenth century, some weaknesses were perceived in the power of Reason and how a Counter-Enlightenment commenced to emerge.

At that time, concerns were expressed at how irreligious and immoral the world could become if everything were to be assessed in the light of cold, intellectual logic.

Hicks remarks that Immanuel Kant was a key player in the Counter-Enlightenment movement.

Kant pointed out that there is no guarantee that all our reason, all our cognitive faculties, will lead us to discover objective reality. Kant was a religious person and wanted to give reason the place it deserved, but no more. He wanted to ensure there was a place for faith.

However, by acknowledging that our finite cognitive capacities can give us a distorted image of objective reality, Kant, unfortunately, redefined truth on subjective grounds, and in the words of Stephen Hicks, *"Kant was the decisive break with the Enlightenment and the first major step towards postmodernism."*[xxi]

Following Kant, Hegel posited that although reason allows us to discover some reality, our understanding of reality is always going to be limited, not only because we are facing contradictions (for example, the world is made of simple parts but at the same time it is complex), but also because we do not accept that reality can be contradictory, such as, for instance (this writer's illustration), the biblical concept of the Trinity in which God is one and at the same time three different Persons.

Hegel thought that we would forever live in a world of contradictions so that contradictions would span across eras and centuries and hence *"what is metaphysically and epistemologically true in one epoch will be contradicted by what is true in the next, and so on."*[xxii]

It follows, therefore, that absolute truth does not exist. What is absolutely true in one era could be absolutely untrue in another.

The loss of absolute truth is the first seed that gave birth to our present catastrophic state of affairs.

What next?

Following Kant and Hegel, the Danish philosopher Kierkegaard moves us away from the world of reason and contradictory reason into the realm of irrationalism; Kierkegaard believed indeed that since not everything could be discovered or proven by reason, an irrational leap of faith was required on the part of Man, a typical illustration of which is the biblical account of the botched killing of Isaac by his father, Abraham.

All this paved the way for the eventual collapse of Reason in the twentieth century: our second seed.

Enters then Martin Heidegger

Heidegger was an early twentieth-century German philosopher who refused to have his thinking dominated by logic. He thought reason and logic were superficial elements that prevented us from finding meaning. So, in contrast to cold logic and reasoning, Heidegger emphasises the role of emotions and, particularly boredom, fear, guilt and dread. Coupled with his negative emotions, this particular type of thinking led Heidegger to believe that all is nothing and nothing is all.

In other words, nihilism.

Nothing is sacred but nothing is profane; neither exists and therefore, in the famous words of Frederick Nietzsche, "God is dead".

Meanwhile, no absolute truth, no absolute lie.

Nihilism: the third seed.

Nihilists see nothing but an absurd world which makes no sense, as postulated by the early twentieth-century members of the existentialist school, Jean-Paul Sartre, Albert Camus and Simone de Beauvoir.

An absurd world, Sartre explains, also brought about by the pressures placed on us by a society that creates conformity and therefore alienates us from our authenticity, from being true to ourselves.

A perpetual conflict between what we do under constraint and who we really are.

A constant search for our authentic self, which presumes the discovery of who we are through an identity that is not necessarily approved of or recognised by society and yet is supposedly vital to the attainment of full human potential and fulfilment.

The search for the authentic self … Here is the fourth seed and maybe the most important of all, for it is indeed this search for the authentic that offered Left-wing intellectuals the strategic turning point they had been looking for to regain the upper ground.

The Left, indeed, originally was the embodiment of the opposition of the poor against the rich.

The French Revolution of 1789 supports this.

The nobles, the king and the clergy all had a privileged lifestyle, but the general populace was poor, ill-educated and lacking in the necessities of life.

The French Revolution was, therefore the uprising of the poor against the rich, which eventually gave rise to the slogan Liberty, Equality and Fraternity.

Likewise, Karl Marx's major work *Das Kapital* was a work of the Left, postulating an ongoing struggle between the proletariat and the privileged with the aim of creating a better society "from each according to his ability to each according to his need".

However, the great uprising of the increasingly numerous proletariat in the Western World never materialised for the simple reason that more became rich and less became poor, so communism as an economic model simply failed.

The Left then had to re-invent itself and started to look at other battlefields than those of the economic ground. The fourth seed to our current state of affairs was the launching pad of this re-invention. The search for the authentic self. The rejection of the superfluous and the superficial, which were seen to be portrayed in the "bourgeois" values of the late 50s became the new target. The 1960s' catch cry "make love, not war" was the epithet of a culture that started to value free love, devalue traditional marriage and shied away from orthodox career paths.

The events that occurred at the Sorbonne University in Paris in 1968 typified the new culture of the day.

Students occupied La Sorbonne in May 1968 originally as a protest against the Vietnam War, but the revolt soon spread to the country in its entirety as workers' unions, dissatisfied with the employment conditions of the time, engineered a massive strike across the entire nation.

The hippy culture that had originated in the US as a moral opposition to the war in Vietnam soon spread across Europe.

France, which had been a bastion of conservative culture, was not overlooked.

The youth of 1968 were tired of the atrocities of the Second World War, which had been recounted to them by their parents; it was also barely six years since France had ended the war in Algeria, therefore relinquishing 130 years of colonial rule in that part of the world. Furthermore, the violence in Vietnam was clearly felt at the time as a manifestation of another attempt at conserving the imperialism culture of the Western World.

The German American philosopher, Herbert Marcuse, had a profound influence on the cultural revolution of the 60s and believed that a different type of alienation or oppression was exercised over the populace by the owners of capital. No longer was it economic oppression but rather an oppression of what it meant to be human. With the industrial revolution and commodification of Western Society, Marcuse thought that Man was becoming more of a machine, or at least a cog in the machine, and was losing the essence of his humanity.

His contribution and that of others in the Frankfurt School

were paramount to the development of Critical Theory, the very philosophy that became the foundational plank of the current plague: postmodernism.

The New Left was then born – no longer in opposition to the economic poor against the privileged rich but rather in opposition to the cultural heritage of the Western World, its materialism, its strict moral code and cultural norms.

Respect for authority diminished; alternative lifestyles spread and were typified in the "hippy commune". The morality of previous generations started to be questioned; living together as a trial exercise for marriage became acceptable; the Church lost authority.

University entrance became more accessible – in Australia under the Whitlam government, there was a period of free university education available to all who qualified to attend on academic grounds. In most of Europe, and particularly in France, university was considered a logical progression beyond high school and was free of charge.

The prevalence of university education fostered a role for debate and debating societies. The New Left became the champion of a new mentality that took hold, in part, due to an increasing number of students enrolling in humanities or Arts degrees.

The search for authenticity, the rally cry of Sartre and de Beauvoir, challenged the intelligentsia of the time as to how we could even <u>know</u> what is truly authentic.

This was so, at least until another Frenchman and La Sorbonne academic, Michel Foucault, developed a new theory of knowledge.

Foucault's understanding of knowledge was based on his appreciation of the concept of power.

For Foucault, power was everywhere. It prevailed in everything. It prevailed, therefore, also in language or discourse.

According to Foucault, the power of discourse is found in the cultural background of the speaker, and the knowledge element that discourse contains is never absolute because it is influenced by the relativism of culture.

Hence discourse needs to be deconstructed to arrive at the true meaning of the knowledge it claims to proclaim.

So where are we?

Reason no longer exists, life is absurd, there is no absolute truth, there is no true knowledge, and everything needs to be deconstructed to ascertain the cultural prejudices hidden in discourse. We are still in despair. The God-is-dead movement is still alive; nihilism prevails, be in it a modified form.

In fact, we have most probably fallen further down into the abyss.

Insecurity therefore abounds – insecurity not only about the purpose of existence but the insecurity of everyday life. The insecurity of employment, of financial sufficiency, of physical and mental health. The insecurity of what is in store for the next generation.

Where are we then left to go?

In the words of Stephen Hicks again:

> *"We can, as the conservatives would prefer, simply turn to our groups' traditions and follow them. Or we can, as the post-modernists would prefer, turn to our feelings and follow them… From Kierkegaard and Heidegger, we learn that our emotional core is a deep sense of dread and guilt. From Marx, we feel a deep sense of alienation, victimization, and rage. From Nietzsche, we discover a deep need for power. From Freud, we uncover the urgings of dark and aggressive sexuality. Rage, power, guilt, lust and dread constitute the centre of the postmodern emotional universe."*[xxiii]

So, there is no need to be logical and consistent anymore. We can have borders without having borders. We can have males who are not males and females who are not females. We can have discourse without meaning. We can have meaning without sense and so on.

It also follows that since reason and objective knowledge have been brushed away, judgment is no longer relevant. To judge something as unreasonable makes no sense if reason does not exist.

This is why one of the key tenets of the woke postmodern philosophy is its rejection of anything that sounds judgmental.

Unfortunately, a society that does not allow its members to judge encourages a trend away from being discerning, a trend away from sharing opinions, from engaging in debate. It brings up fences, borders which isolate us in our own world. It entrenches us more in our viewpoints. Hence the perverse consequence of postmodernism.

By banning judgment, it aims to encourage broadmindedness, but, instead, it produces the opposite outcome: we become more opiniated, immovable in our thinking because we do not hear or welcome an opposite view that could challenge or judge our values.

We have become an endangered species, a civilisation on the brink, blinded by its intellectual short-sightedness, unable to think independently.

One of the major threats we are facing is indoctrination, and this issue will be examined in Chapter 5.

However, before closing the present chapter, we should not overlook that one of the major reasons we have landed where we are today is due to the rise of sexual identity and that much of that is owed to Sigmund Freud (1856-1939).

Carl Trueman writes that "*Freud has, in fact, provided the West with a compelling myth… the idea that sex, in terms of sexual desire and sexual fulfillment, is the real key to human existence, to what it means to be human.'[xxiv]*

In his book *The Rise and Triumph of the Modern Self,* Trueman explains that Freud is the logical progression to the rise of the "psychological man", a type that focuses on feelings, beauty, and happiness. This was initiated largely by the French and English romantic poets of the 19th century, but Freud takes it to a new level, so to speak, by promoting the concept that true happiness lies in the satisfaction of sexual desire.

To wit and quote:

> *"Man's discovery that sexual genital love afforded him the strongest experiences of satisfaction and in fact provided him with the prototype of all happiness, must have suggested to him that he should continue to seek the satisfaction of happiness in his life along the path of sexual relations and that he should make genital erotism the central point of his life."[xxv]*

Freud was an atheist who considered religion as an infantile neurosis. He, therefore, had no time for Christianity. In fact, he believed that religion causes psychological problems although it had been of service for human civilisation in the past.

Religions frustrate sexual fulfilment which is the core ingredient to achieving happiness.

Consequently, to discover his authentic self, Man has to accept that sexuality defines personhood.

Again, in the words of Carl Trueman, *"before Freud, sex was an activity, for procreation or for recreation; after Freud, sex is definitive of who we are, as individuals, as societies, and as species."[xxvi]*

Summary

The current state of affairs we find ourselves immersed into finds its origins at least as far back as the 18th-century European Enlightenment.

Whereas the Reformation period ushered a religious renewal and a break from the Roman Catholic Church, the Enlightenment focused on Reason and Logic.

An overreliance on Reason to explain all reality gave impetus to the Counter-Enlightenment period when philosophers such as Hegel postulated that what is metaphysically and epistemologically true in one epoch will be contradicted by what is true in the next.

This caused the demise of the concept of absolute truth. The first seed.

Without absolute truth, Reason no longer ruled supreme. The second seed essential for the rise of emotivism was then sown.

From then on, it was only a short step to nihilism. The third seed. If nothing can be absolutely true, how can anything make actual sense?

This brought in a sense of despair and absurdity from which Western Europe eventually extricated itself (but only in part) following Jean Paul Sartre's search for the authentic self in the first half of the 20th century.

This search for the authentic – the fourth seed – was the launch of a new movement for the Left. With increasing living standards and relative opulence, the old economic communism of Marx fell into disrepute. The Left then had to "reinvent" itself, searching for what is really true and authentic outside the religious faith of its elders.

This search for what is authentic in a world that denies God continues to haunt our current identity-focused generation of the 21st century, which in turn also suffers from the legacy of Sigmund Freud.

Sexual desire and sexual fulfilment are, therefore, now the basis of most identities.

Control over the choice of one's gender and sexuality has become the key to discovering the authentic self.

Chapter 4

Water Pour

In the previous chapter, we explained that four seeds were sown to grow and produce the current fruit of our new culture.

The loss of absolute truth was the first seed; the loss of Reason was the second; nihilism was the third, and the search for the authentic, the fourth.

However, seeds do not grow well unless they are watered well.

So, what sort of water made these seeds of cultural destruction grow?

An important "water pour" on these seeds is the rise of a new atheism.

Until fairly recently, atheism was simply a philosophical conviction that God does not exist. There was no judgment attached to that philosophy. The God-is-dead movement was largely comprised of philosophers who simply believed that there is no God. Darwin, in his famous book, *The Origins of Species,* made his case for evolution and opposed anyone who believed in a divine Creator. His work was further developed by others who gave us a variety of explanations, such as, for instance, the Big Bang Theory. But until the 20th century, atheism remained a philosophical position largely devoid of moral judgement on those who held religious beliefs.

With the rise of the New Atheists, all this started to change.

The key figures in the New Atheism movement are Richard Dawkins, Sam Harris, the late Christopher Hitchens and Daniel Dennett.

The principal message conveyed by these four philosophers is a refinement of Freud's views on religion.

For the new atheists, all religion (maybe with the exception of Buddhism) is inimical to happiness and freedom of thought and expression.

By depicting all religions as the source of dissension, the New Atheists refuse to acknowledge the existence of any peaceful religion and thereby express a great ignorance or at least misunderstanding of Christian theology.

This position is, therefore, a declaration of war against the historical religious background of a nation such as Australia; it has fuelled the "cancel culture" movement which we discussed in an earlier chapter.

However, a second "water pour" over our four seeds was the relatively recent rise of a terrorist version of the Islamic faith and the revelations of sexual abuse perpetrated in some sections of the Catholic and other churches.

This gave religion even more of a bad name and provided further ammunition to the New Atheists.

Furthermore, much of the opposition made by the New Atheists is also a reaction to a more distant historical development, which unfortunately has been misnamed the Christian Right.

The Christian Right should not be confused with the fascist ideas of the Nazi movement that duped some sections of the German Christian church in the 1930s into believing that Jews and homosexuals should be exterminated.

The Christian Right, which for a while was also referred to under the more acceptable label of the Moral Majority, started approximately 50 years ago in the United States.

The following article published by the Association of Religion Data Archives (ARDA) gives a good précis of its origins.

> *"During the 1970s, conservative Catholics and evangelical Protestants became increasingly worried about the moral direction of the United States. The U.S. Supreme Court had banned official prayers in public schools, upheld abortion rights, and protected free speech for pornographers. Moreover, the popular though ultimately unsuccessful movement to pass the Equal Rights Amendment for women's equality in the workplace seemed to undermine the traditional family and male authority. Popular evangelical authors like Francis Schaeffer warned that these decisions were the fruit of a campaign by "secular humanists" to transform America from its true origins as a Christian nation. Schaeffer and other conservative intellectuals called for a mass response from evangelical Christians who had been traditionally reluctant to engage in electoral politics. In the late 1970s, however, they responded, and a loose network of conservative Christian advocacy groups – including the Christian Voice, the Moral Majority, the Religious Roundtable, and the National Christian Action Coalition – were formed. These groups were at the centre of the movement that academics later labelled the New Christian Right."* [xxvii]

The movement spread from the United States to Australia and has been unfairly and increasingly criticised by secular political movements for its fundamentalism.

The label "Christian right" is not something this writer endorses because it has pejorative connotations associated with fascism, and it does not depict any of the Christian political movements in Australia. It is fundamentalist in its theology but not revolutionary and certainly accepts that Australia is a democratic country.

I would prefer to rename the movement the Conservative Christian voice.

The Conservative Christian voice in Australia regroups a number of institutions.

The Christian Democratic Party (which has now disbanded) was a party established in New South Wales, previously under the name of Call to Australia. It was the first Christian party launched in Australia. It was established in 1977 and a high-profile Christian minister, Reverend Fred Nile, was elected to the Legislative Council of the New South Wales Parliament in 1981.

Other conservative Christian political parties or movements in Australia include the Australian Christian Party, The Family First Party, the Australian Christian Lobby, the National Civic Council, the Democratic Labor Party and the Australian Family Association, to name but a few.

All these Christian parties or associations in Australia are focused on pro-family and pro-life policies, which places them in direct opposition with the New Atheism movement, which opposes all political, conservative family platforms.

To sum up, the key water source that allowed our four seeds to grow has been the rise of the New Atheism galvanised, on the one hand, by the opposition of a rising Conservative Christian voice (comprised of a number of pro-traditional family Christian parties/movements), but also propelled, on the other hand, by the cumulative effects of a terrorist version of the Islamic religion and of a large-scale sexual abuse perpetrated in some sections of the Catholic church.

Most importantly, the New Atheism movement has been particularly effective in facilitating a rapid growth of the fourth seed, the authentic self.

By discrediting the values of the traditional family and of religion in general, the New Atheists have removed much of the life purpose offered by the institutions of church and family to previous Australian generations. To have a meaningful life, it is essential to have some sense of purpose or mission, and the search for the authentic self, initially launched by Jean-Paul Sartre and Simone de Beauvoir, has now unfortunately taken a new direction: the search for group identity.

The desire to belong to a specific group, tribe or clan, has always been part of the human psyche. However, the degree of intensity now expressed in bearing a specific group identity label is something new.

It is no longer a private individual quest but now a political movement supported by the media, the teaching institutions and the corporate world.

My view is that the search-for-identity political movement is also fuelled by a growing sense of psychological alienation among the younger generation.

We are living in a world of high pressure:
- Pressure to compete
- Pressure to succeed, be it at school or at university or in the marketplace.
- Pressure to acquire economic security
- Pressure to acquire or retain employment.
- Pressure also for social acceptance and recognition.

Everything seems to be driven by competition, by some sort of race for an eluding trophy of self-preservation – a lot of "me versus the world" type of feeling.

Hence the sense of alienation and the search for group support where like-minded creatures can find some sense of solidarity, encouragement and possibly, then, purpose.

This sense of alienation would also be fuelled by a view that the role of government is primarily to provide me with the safety I need.

Indeed, whereas in previous times, many perceived that the role of government was largely limited to the provision of law and order, there is now a growing consensus that the government is here to provide for my personal safety.

However, the definition of safety has been changed and safety no longer just means safety from physical harm but safety from all harms, including emotional harm.

Naturally, this is an impossible task for any government to accomplish, nor should any government be expected to do so, but the failures to legislate comprehensively in this regard only accentuate the feeling of alienation of the present generation.

It is, therefore, natural that groups that are formed to offer a refuge shelter to an alienated mankind become more politically active and strident in their claims to protect specific identities from emotional harm.

These groups seek to obtain recognition of a new morality by legislative fiat (based on a new definition of "harm").

They want legislative recognition of the victimhood they suffer due to their alienation from the broader society.

They are creating a new morality, and to quote Jonathan Haidt: morality binds and blinds.

> *"Morality binds and blinds. It binds us into ideological teams that fight each other as though the fate of the world depended on our side winning each battle. It blinds us to the fact that each team is composed of good people who have something important to say".* [xxviii]

Haidt explains that our society is being separated largely into two camps, conservative and progressive or "liberals" to use his American terminology.

He believes these two groups do not communicate properly because they have different moralities and do not attempt to understand each other. Instead, they caricature each other.

Passions are riding so high in politics that reasoning no longer applies. Intuitions dictate.

Labor and Green voters in Australia will intuitively believe that anything that a Liberal government will do in future will be harmful. Likewise, Liberal voters will fail to see that Labor can at times also provide sound, moral decisions.

This is, of course, amplified in the way parliamentary debates are conducted in this country.

There is hardly ever a recognition that the other side might have it right. The job of the Opposition is to oppose and to oppose at all costs. There is no balance in the process.

Although this style of parliamentary debate has always existed, what is new is that it is now mirrored in our society at large.

In addition, there is also now a greater sense of distrust in established institutions.

People feel alienated and forgotten but forgotten in a very different sense from what Prime Minister Menzies meant when he made his famous speech about the forgotten people.

Menzies was talking about the middle class in his speech about the forgotten people.

Today, those who feel alienated comprise some in the middle class, many in the academic institutions, and some more in the "chattering classes".

The culture wars also alienate the conservative · thinkers further away from the New Left.

Menzies would have been very wary of the huge reliance on the emotions, intuitions and the like, expressed by the woke movement nowadays in its staunch opposition to what has been, until now, known as Western civilisation.

Menzies encouraged thinking and he wanted all of us to think, middle class, working class and upper class.

He wrote:

> *"The moment a man seeks moral and intellectual refuge in the emotions of a crowd, he ceases to be a human being and becomes a cipher."* [xxix]

We will return to this and examine in a later chapter how our way of thinking is increasingly depictive of a herd mentality and of the indoctrination threats we are facing as a nation.

At this juncture, let us now consider in more depth what may be termed 'a culture of victimhood'.

Summary

The four seeds at the origin of our present state of affairs were cultivated and well-watered by a number of sociological events which contributed to the transformation of our society.

The rise of the New Atheist movement spearheaded by Richard Dawkins, Sam Harris, Christopher Hitchens and Daniel Dennett painted all religions as significant sources of dissension and dangerous philosophies that needed to be destroyed.

The Judeo-Christian ethics, which until then had been the principal pillars of Australian society, started to be replaced by the aggressive "cancel culture" that surrounds us today.

This onslaught was also facilitated by the abusive practices conducted in a number of Christian churches and more particularly in the Roman Catholic Church.

The nation's quest for meaning and purpose, formerly found in faith and religious practices, then took a new direction with an increasing focus placed on what is authentic at the level of the individual.

The concept of the psychological man, initially promoted by Freud, took prominence with an inevitable focus on gender and sexuality.

The resistance offered by the conservative wing of the Christian church and by a number of Christian political activists unfortunately only galvanised the New Atheist movement further.

Society became unstable and, coupled with economic pressure, new popular expectations arose. A sizeable portion of the Australian population turned to the government to provide them with the security they had lost; a sense of alienation emerged.

Constant attention to the self has become a narcissistic obsession at the base of a new culture of victimhood and a renewed sense of oppression among the younger generations.

Chapter 5

A Culture of Victimhood

Woke postmodernism sees everyone and everything through the lens of victimhood.

Even the oppressor is a victim of the culture in which he has been brought up: he is captive, prisoner to his own cultural conditioning.

Furthermore, this victimhood mentality is strongly reinforced by the continuous usage of the new woke word "microaggression".

Microaggressions are those tiny traumas inflicted through the use of plain, otherwise inoffensive language that is perceived to be highly offensive by the recipient.

This fairly new sociological development has been the subject of a detailed study by leading US academics Bradley Campbell and Jason Manning.

In their book *"The Rise of Victimhood Culture"*xxx, these authors explain how the current culture of victimhood follows up the demise of the cultures of dignity and honour that prevailed in former times in Western society, thereby vindicating this author's view that postmodernism does not uphold human dignity.

> *"In honour cultures, it is one's reputation that makes*
> *one honourable or not, and one must respond aggressively*
> *to insults, aggressions and challenges or else lose honour*
> *.... Cultures of honour tend to arise in places where legal*

authority is weak or non-existent and where a reputation
for toughness is perhaps the only effective deterrent."[xxxi]

Honour cultures were, therefore, those, for instance, where an insulted gentleman responded by inviting his opponent to a duel.

On the other hand, dignity cultures are more in the line of the "stiff upper lip" type, which has been popularised particularly in more conservative Anglo-Saxon circles.

As Campbell and Manning point out, '*dignity exists independently from what others think, so a culture of dignity is one in which public reputation is less important. Insults might provoke offense, but they no longer have the same impact as a way of establishing or destroying a reputation."*[xxxii]

In a dignity culture, the offended party considers himself to be above the insult and will not condescend in humiliating himself by acknowledging the insult.

However, we no longer live among cultures of honour or dignity. We no longer feel that our reputation can be preserved if we avenge our honour in mortal combat. Nor do we feel we should keep a "stiff upper lip". No, today, the consensus among the woke elites is that we can condemn the perceived aggressor, if not always through the bias of judicial channels, at least publicly through the media, particularly the social media and the organised campaigns of sympathetic or co-belligerent woke militants.

We are self-professed victims seeking redress through external channels (social media, press, courts, and legislature).

The question then is why did we transit from honour to dignity and then to victimhood?

Naturally, this has not occurred overnight, and the reasons are complex.

On the one hand, there are educational influences at play. On the other, there is also this sentiment that we live in an unjust world. Social justice activists campaign by promoting situational examples of injustice through a largely diffused public media with the principal aim of incensing and shocking a malleable public into thinking that the authorities are the source of all unfairness and injustice.

Ironically, they often seek assistance from these same authorities to give a veneer of justice to their claims. The Australian Human Rights Commission has often been appealed to when offense is claimed. A recent well-known case was the QUT and Callum Thwaites case.[4]

This organised systemic promotion of victimhood is the reason why we can now call it a culture.

Victimhood is very politically correct because, in a society that only perceives two categories, aggressors and victims, nobody wants to be labelled an aggressor. Therefore, only one choice arises: victimhood.

My view is that part of the victimhood mentality is grounded in the pervasive sense of social injustice or alienation we discussed in the previous chapter.

Most likely, the impact of the public service bureaucracies (and the potential for deserving applicants to fall "between the cracks" of established welfare programs) contributes to this state of affairs. There is also a sense of "missing out" compared with the older generations. For instance, real estate in Australia is rapidly becoming unaffordable to the young and reliance on debt becomes more necessary than it was in the last century.

Generation Y, brought up in relative opulence by their Boomer parents, now look to the State for distributive justice and remain disappointed by what they consider a poor level of support.

---

[4] https://aip.asn.au/newsletter/tony-morris-and-calum-thwaites/?frame=0

There is, therefore, a sense of disenchantment, of disappointed and negative thinking prevailing among some of our younger people.

A sense of entitlement (albeit not necessarily always justified) is at the root of a negative outlook on society and the future.

In some sense, therefore, Generation Y feels that it is the victim of the economic success of its forebears.

This sense of alienation is part and parcel of the conflict in which the woke elites are now engaged.

In some ways, it is an expression of the revolutionary rite of passage to adulthood, but it is also very new in the sense that there is a stronger sense of solidarity among the perceived oppressed. It is also much more permanent, more entrenched, than any past generational "revolutionary rite of passage."

In this regard, it is worth noting that Dr Rahav Gabay of Tel Aviv University developed a new personality trait category: Tendency for Interpersonal Victimhood (TPV),[xxxiii] the main characteristics of which were aptly summarised in a journal article in the Scientific American under the title of *Unravelling the Mindset of Victimhood.*[xxxiv]

This article explained that TPV is "*an ongoing feeling that the self is a victim, which is generalized across many kinds of relationships*" and that "*based on clinical observations and research, the researchers found that the tendency for interpersonal victimhood consists of four main dimensions: (a) constantly seeking recognition for one's victimhood, (b) moral elitism, (c) lack of empathy for the pain and suffering of others, and (d) frequently ruminating about past victimization.*"

These four dimensions are foundational to the mentality of the woke elites. They see themselves as morally superior because they belong to the camp of the oppressed (or at least express verbal sympathy for the oppressed); they repeat over and over again the same mantra of lamentations concerning the injustices perpetrated by the so-called Western civilisation and they have no empathy for those outside their particular identity niche.

In an article published in the European Journal of Social Psychology, Nora Schori-Eyal takes this further. She discusses another aspect of the problem of victimhood: "Perpetual ingroup victimhood."[xxxv]

Perpetual ingroup victimhood (PIV) is a permanent expression of group-based victimhood.

Schori-Eyal reminds us that group-based victimhood is *"the perception of the ingroup as having suffered severe, intentional and unjust harm at the hands of another group or groups."*

Some of the consequences of this type of victimhood include *"reduced willingness to acknowledge ingroup responsibility for moral violation... less support for intergroup forgiveness and reconciliation... consolidation of societal beliefs in the justness of the ingroup's goals. delegitimization of the rival. general outgroup mistrust and support for exclusion ... (and) decreased empathy towards outgroups."*

Group-based victimhood has traditionally focused on the behaviour of national, ethnic or religious groups (for instance, Jews versus Palestinians), but as Schori-Eyal points out, one feature of the mindset is that *"the harm incurred by the ingroup has not been a single, transitory, or accidental experience but rather an enduring reality caused intentionally by a determined enemy or even a succession of enemies."*

As a subset of group-based victimhood, Schori-Eyal tells us that *"PIV is unique in linking past and present: the historical injustices incurred by the ingroup may have taken place many centuries in the past but still impact the attitudes, emotions and behaviours of contemporary group members throughout the belief that past enemies are reincarnated in current adversaries ... the group (then becomes) disposed or is even destined to be victimized by others."*

This is exactly what Critical Theory is all about: it is grounded on perceived injustices perpetrated over many centuries through Western culture colonisation, be it of a geographical, educational or moral nature.

The outgroup is considered a permanent foe, a constant adversary who gives rise to the concept of a "repugnant cultural other", a phrase coined by anthropologist Susan Harding.[xxxvi].

Although the concept Harding developed was initially in connection with a study on Christian fundamentalism (in the context of the early 20th-century debate in the US between creationists and evolutionists), it is perfectly symptomatic of how the woke elites consider Western civilisation: racist and oppressive. The Western world is, therefore, culturally repugnant!

This repugnance arises from a distorted caricature of the outgroup. It is the reflection of a fundamentalist ideological movement at war against any other form of fundamentalism.

Morality

Such repugnance arises as each side considers the other to be immoral and it blocks communication.

In the current culture wars, the woke elite not only considers Western civilisation to be immoral but indeed, it now uses a totally new language of morality.

The old moral language, which included terms with positive connotations such as loyalty, authority, respect, self-sacrifice etc, is now being substituted by a completely new lexicon of negative terms such as microassault, microinsult, microinvalidation, mansplaining, whitesplaining, straightsplaining, fat shaming, cultural appropriation etc.

In their book on the culture of victimhood, Campbell & Manning refer to a "17-page Diversity and Social Glossary created by the Diversity Resource Centre at the University of Washington, Tacoma.[xxxvii.]

The consequences of this new morality are devastating on our ability to communicate intelligently but also on how to think.

The woke elites' thinking is largely negative, pessimistic and protectionist. Intellectual progress is therefore hindered through a prism that considers that progress cannot be achieved unless a completely new type of society is established. In order to advance, one must first destroy.

In the woke world, nothing is safe. The other is the enemy and thinking is directed first of all at how to create safe spaces.

Hence, language definitions are expanded to give more room to the emotional dimension. So, for instance, whereas violence and abuse were formerly physical acts, frequent mention is now made of emotional abuse and emotional violence.

The influence of the Internet on the expansion of a victimhood culture is also considerable.

Groups of influence are no longer limited to friends, colleagues, and students but very much also to the encounters one can make in 'chat rooms' who push only a particular point of view.

This is particularly the case with regard to the new transgender crisis.

Teenagers looking for support for their self-perceived victimisation are not offered impartial advice on the Internet, with a list of pros and cons, so to speak. No words of caution, no mention of medical or psychological risks, of those who had regrets or even of those who sought to de-transition.

Wall Street journalist, Abigail Shrier, has studied the issue of transgenderism in depth and published a book titled *Irreversible Damage- Teenager Girls and the Transgender Craze*. It is not a book expressing hatred towards the transgender. Rather, it is a book denouncing the little encouragement made to consider intellectually, rather than just emotionally what transgenderism really offers.

Here is some of what she has to say on the subject:

> "There are more than a dozen social media sites and online forums that facilitate the discovery of a trans identity. YouTube, Instagram, Tumble, Reddit, Twitter, Facebook, DeviantArt and TikTok are all popular hubs for sharing and documenting a physical transformation, seething over transphobia, celebrating the superpowers conferred by testosterone, offering tips for procuring a prescription, and commiserating about how hard it is to be trans today.
>
> "Trans influencers have a few classic mantras. Here's some of the advice you are likely to receive from them:
>
> 1) if you think you might be trans, you are;
>
> 2) (breast) binders are a great way to start;
>
> 3) testosterone or "T" is amazing, it may just solve all your problems;
>
> 4) if your parents loved you, they would support your identity;
>
> 5) if you are not supported in your trans identity, you'll probably kill yourself.
>
> 6) deceiving parents and doctors is justified if it helps transition;
>
> 7) you don't have to identify as the opposite sex to be "trans". "xxxviii.

These social media influencers have a huge influence; for instance, Shrier names an Ash Ardell who believes her authentic identity is something between male and female. Shrier says that she has over 650,000 YouTube subscribers.[xxxix]

Moral injury

The concept of moral injury is at the core of the new victimhood morality culture.

Moral injury has been defined as "*the profound psychological distress which results from actions, or the lack of them which violates one's moral or ethical code.*"[xl]

To date, the discussion of moral injury has largely revolved around the state of returned soldiers who have been confronted with the atrocities of war, front-line key workers such as healthcare providers, and ambulance officers.

However, the rise of the victimhood culture now demands a new definition of what constitutes 'moral injury'.

Can the perception of repeated microaggressions result in the "profound psychological distress" that has characterised moral injury to date?

And if the answer is affirmative, how do we treat it?

The answer to this question, of course, is outside the scope of this book, but it must nevertheless be raised if we are to achieve progress as a nation.

Summary

In past centuries, honour and dignity cultures prevailed. These cultures have now been displaced, and instead, we now live a culture of victimhood.

This culture of victimhood is typified by what sociologists have now called "microaggression".

Microaggressions are those tiny traumas inflicted through the use of plain, otherwise inoffensive language that is perceived to be highly offensive by the recipient.

A number of factors have contributed to the development of this new perception of reality. We live in an insecure world where the individual craves recognition and where narcissism is on the rise; self-centredness abounds.

A pervasive sense of disenchantment and alienation has cast a shadow over our society; this has been fuelled, in part, by an entitlement culture that can never be fully satisfied.

The authorities, the courts, the government are now expected to provide us with not only physical but also emotional safety.

A new personality trait, Tendency for Interpersonal Victimhood (TPV), has been identified by leading sociologists. TPV displays four major features: (1) a constant search for recognition of one's victimhood, (2) moral elitism, (3) a lack of empathy for the pain and suffering of others, and (4) a tendency to ruminate frequently about past victimisation.

These features are the fundamental identity marks of postmodern woke philosophy.

The influence of the Internet on the expansion of a victimhood culture is also considerable.

Groups of influence are no longer limited to friends, colleagues, and students but very much also to the encounters one can make in 'chat rooms' who push only a particular point of view.

A new perception of repeated micro-aggressions might eventually result in the profound psychological distress that will destroy our entire society.

Chapter 6

Fear, Insecurity and Isolation

"A palpable sense of intolerance towards freedom, particularly freedom of speech, is intimately connected to the working of the culture of fear."[xli]

We are living in a culture of fear. There is no doubt about this and by fear, we do not refer to a recent phenomenon fuelled by the COVID-19 pandemic but to an emotion that has overtaken most of Western society, including Australia, for many years now. Worse still, it is growing, and its presence may be detected in all echelons of society.

We are fearful of losing our employment; we are fearful we might get seriously sick; we are fearful of being robbed; we are fearful of retirement, but most importantly, we are now fearful of the reactions of our neighbours and friends and sometimes even of those of our own relatives.

As mentioned in the Preface of this book, we are fragile because we are increasingly traumatised by how others are going to misinterpret our words. We are worried about being "cancelled", ignored, ostracized, and in an effort of self-preservation, we choose to isolate ourselves and not to debate anything that might be seen as controversial, particularly if it is political or religious.

How did we reach such a sad state of affairs?

Renowned sociologist, Frank Furedi, believes that our obsession in seeing the past as a series of bad news conditions us into "representing vulnerability as the eternal condition of life."[xlii]

However, the culture of fear certainly precedes the recent rise of woke philosophy and its total obsession of seeing any cultural past as fundamentally bad. As discussed earlier, following the loss of Reason, Western society moved into an era where emotions became supreme, and, whereas in earlier times, fear was a state to be overcome through courage, it is now a menace that should be avoided at all costs, even if it means deprivation of civil liberties.

One of our problems is that we have lost the ability to assess real versus imaginary risk.

US leading academics, Greg Lukianoff and Jonathan Haidt, have pointed out that we often see much risk in situations where little of it prevails.

In their bestseller work *The Coddling of the American Mind*, they write:

> "*The cities and towns in which the parents of iGen were raised were far more dangerous than they are today. Baby Boomers and Gen-Xers grew up with rising rates of crime and mayhem. Muggings were a normal part of urban life, and city dwellers sometimes carried "muggers' money" in a cheap wallet so they would not have to hand over their real wallets.*"[xliii].

Most Australians are not really aware of this because in the 60s and 70s, we were still much unpopulated and the Commonwealth Government then encouraged mass migration from a number of European countries, such as England, France, Italy, and Greece. Populate or perish was the immigration policy of that era.

Arguably, we were then living in a less dangerous world but only because Australia was less populated than it is now. Yet, it is incorrect to believe that it is the increase in our population that has contributed to an escalation in risk. To some extent, this is true but since Australia is largely influenced by the ideology prevailing in Europe and the United States, it is no surprise that, as is the case for them, we also see much risk where little actually exists.

We hear much about "helicopter parenting", a concept totally foreign to my parents' generation and those who preceded them.

In the words of Lukianoff and Haidt: "*good parents are (now) expected to believe that their children are in danger every moment they are unsupervised*"[xliv].

Paranoid parenting has created a culture of "safetyism" that is now pervasive throughout all of society.

On the other hand, some new and real risks have also now arisen as a result of the greater influence of social media and the ascending acceptance of woke philosophy.

One of these is vilification.

The Oxford dictionary defines vilification as 'abusive disparaging speech or writing.'

Although we have no reason to disagree with this definition, the adjective 'abusive" is now applied to beliefs and actions which are not popular among a certain section of society.

This was not the case before. Abuse in previous generations was the perpetration of acts of misused power, not just the airing of opinions that diverge from someone's personal beliefs.

The Human Rights Law Alliance, an Australian Canberra-based legal firm, writes on its website:

> *There is a low bar for the making and acceptance of vilification complaints.*

> *For example, complaints may be lodged through relatively simple online forms. The wording of the Acts also means that vilification may be alleged to occur*

through any "public act".

The relevant commissions may also accept any complaints which appear to come within the relevant legislation. They do not first determine whether there has actually been a breach.

Despite the low bar, if a complaint is accepted, a respondent may then be subject to the complaints process. The person may be required to attend a compulsory conciliation conference and participate in further negotiations with the complainants. If the complaint is not resolved, it could ultimately be referred for a public tribunal hearing. The respondent may need to attend and give evidence in their(sic) defence at the hearing.

The ease with which a complainant can force a conciliation conference can unhelpfully create an impression that they have a reasonable case and encourage them to pursue the case through to the Tribunal stage when there is no real prospect of success. This can place further burden on the system and takes valuable time and money away from legitimate cases.

This process – occurring before any breach of an Act is even established – is unfortunately like a punishment in and of itself. Even if a vilification complaint is not ultimately successful, a respondent to a complaint may expend significant time, cost and effort in defending the complaint and obtaining legal advice. The process may also be unfamiliar and stressful.

This is particularly concerning in the context of everyday Australians being made the subject of vilification complaints for simply expressing their opinions. The laws are apparently being misused against *such people with beliefs against mainstream views or ideologies.*

With such a low bar for the making and acceptance of complaints, more and more people may find themselves in this position. They too may find themselves 'punished' by the process, even if any complaints against them are ultimately unsuccessful.[xlv]

It is not surprising then that many are now fearful of engaging in debate or publishing unpopular views that might land them in court.

Yet, if we want things to change, we need to speak; we cannot live in fear forever. We need to fight for our freedom of speech and written expression.

Meanwhile, fear is part of the new moral culture. To the extent that morality defines good and immorality bad, fear is now part of the new morality because it is considered good to be fearful. Fear is no longer something we should try to conquer because it is bad. On the contrary, nowadays, fear is good because by expressing it, you point out that you are on the side of the oppressed.

Fear has become part of the weaponry of anti-democratic politics. One unambiguous example is the words of climate campaigner Greta Thunberg. On 25 January, Thunberg gave a speech at the World Economic Forum in Davos. She warned the global leaders: "I don't want you to be hopeful. I want you to panic. I want you to feel the fear I feel every day. And then I want you to act. I want you to act as you would in a crisis. I want you to act as if the house was on fire[5]"

Let us remember, indeed, that as discussed at the beginning

---

[5]

https://en.wikipedia.org/wiki/Speeches_of_Greta_Thunberg#:~:text=On%2025%20January%20Thunberg%20gave,fear%20I%20feel%20every%20day.

of this book, there are only two types of people according to the new woke philosophy: the oppressor and the oppressed. The oppressed, which is largely composed of the new Left, are fearful of the culture which the so-called oppressor, aka the conservative establishment, has created. They are the victims of the old culture. They want to "cancel" this culture because they are fearful of it. Consequently, they forge for themselves a new victim identity. They promote this new "good and moral" identity and create the culture of victimhood we discussed earlier.

Victimhood is now largely learnt, which means fear is also learnt. It is learnt not only among the so-called oppressed class but among the conservative classes as well.

Campbell and Manning recall that Jonathan Haidt *"relates experiences with students at elite high schools who already live in fear of giving offense to recognised victim groups and being referred to what they call the "diversity police"– the school's multicultural centre.'*[xlvi]

A significant danger posed by the new morality of fear is that it encourages governments and administrations to justify their actions through the spread of fear rather than through the power of persuasion and logic.

When it comes to complicated issues, such as that posed by Brexit a few years ago, it is much easier for governments to win the popular war by focusing on emotions rather than logic. Both sides use it. The fear of losing your nation's sovereignty to Brussels is played by the pro-exit camp, the fear of economic devastation upon exiting the Union is played by the pro-EU camp.

It is interesting to note that despite the increasing level of education generally imparted in our society at all levels, be it through school, university or training and professional development, governments tend to look at people as being incapable of making logical, reasoned decisions. They consider that their constituents are only capable of reacting to emotions. What is then more powerful than fear to persuade someone to adopt a particular viewpoint?

The problem with fear is that it can be irrational and therefore defy any logical debate or argumentation.

How do you then preserve, promote and foster intellectual debate and discussion? How do you foster a thinking nation?

How do you also preserve democracy?

If I fear being heard, how can I put my viewpoint forward? If I cannot put my viewpoint forward, how do I contribute to the development of a democratic culture?

A culture of fear, unfortunately, contributes to a culture of indoctrination, a major tool used by the woke movement and to which we will now turn our attention.

Summary

We live in a culture of fear, and we teach our children how to become prone to fear.

Both the general public and the government authorities alike are focused on eliminating risk from our lives. As a result, we sometimes see danger where there is none.

To be fearful is rapidly becoming a laudable quality.

In particular, paranoid parenting has created a culture of "safetyism" that is now pervasive throughout all of society.

At the same time, some real new risks have arisen which dampen our inclination to be heard or even seen. These risks contribute to the silencing, fragilisation and isolation of many Australians.

In particular, the risk of being accused of vilification is rapidly becoming a real threat in conservative circles.

Current vilification laws place a low bar for access to remedy and often result in creating more division than unity in our present Australian society.

As a result, victimhood is now largely learnt, which means fear is also learnt. It is learnt not only among the so-called oppressed class but among the conservative classes as well.

Governments and administrative bodies have exhibited a tendency to exploit fear to justify their policies and actions and have jettisoned the power of persuasion and logic.

Once fear starts inhibiting calm and reasoned debate, the incentive to think rapidly disappears. However, without thinking, without debate, without opinions being heard, without fear of reprisal in the "marketplace", democracy soon ceases to exist.

The dominating culture – those who can impose fear – now prevail. We have completed "full circle" and are now positioned back from where the woke movement wanted to shift us. The only difference is the actors have changed.

As the French are fond of saying: *"plus ça change, plus c'est la même chose"*[6].

---

[6] The more things change, the more they are the same

Chapter 7

Undue Influence

He alone who owns the youth, gains the future

(Adolf Hitler).

We will make the claim that our society is being unduly influenced, call it "brainwashed" if you wish, through multiple agencies: the media, the institutions of learning, the political establishment, the courts and the corporate sector.

This level of undue influence is so pervasive and so focused on its unity of message that it has also started to infiltrate the Christian church.

The weapon of choice used is the appeal to the emotions – appeal to what all human beings aspire to: justice, fairness and love and yet, very cleverly, very subtly, redefine the meanings of these values or, if you prefer, present these values in terms of a wolf in sheep's clothing. It is worth noting that the wolf in sheep's clothing was the original coat of arms of the Fabian Society, which was the elitist forerunner of the radical socialist Left.

The Fabian modus operandi was, like the Roman general Quintus Fabius, that of defeating superior forces by a process of attrition – persistence, harassment and gradual wearing down. It is the preferred "battle plan" of the Left today.

Indeed, the concepts of justice, fairness and love are being redefined through the prism of Critical Race Theory, which we have referred to earlier on under the new buzzword of "wokeism".

The Encyclopedia Britannica records the following entry on Critical Race Theory:

> *"Critical race theory (CRT), the view that the law and legal institutions are inherently racist and that race itself, instead of being biologically grounded and natural, is a socially constructed concept that is used by white people to further their economic and political interests at the expense of people of colour."*[xlvii].

CRT is the prism through which new concepts of justice, fairness and love are being developed and promoted.

The strategy attracts immediate interest and attention. Who indeed is going to claim that he/she does not want to pursue justice, fairness and love? So, the sheep's clothing is attractive but the wolf inside is the claim that all injustice, unfairness and hatred is the fault of the white man.

It is a particularly clever strategy because there is strong historical evidence that white people have perpetrated damage and suffering. There is, therefore, a grain of truth but only one because the fact that people of colour have also perpetuated acts of oppression as violent as those of the white man is conveniently overlooked.[7]

So, the pursuit of justice is painted as an encouragement to

---

[7] It is worth noting that the wolf in sheep's clothing was the original coat of arms of the Fabian Society, which was the elitist forerunner of the radical socialist Left.

The Fabian modus operandi was, like the Roman general Quintus Fabius that of defeating superior forces by a process of attrition – persistence, harassment and gradual wearing down. It is the preferred "battle plan" of the Left today.

redress the acts of oppression of the white man and CRT condemns slavery but it overlooks to say that the African slaves purchased by the Europeans were often already slaves of black men, happy to make money through the sale of their human cargo to the Westerners. Also, it ignores the fact that the Aboriginal tribal wars were already rife before the arrival of the English settlers.

In fact, the practice of slavery has been recorded as far back as 3500 BC in the Sumerian civilisation.

Familiar with the concept of religious indoctrination, the proponents of CRT elevate the movement to the status of a new religion, denouncing the old ones (in particular Christianity) and refusing to entertain any argumentation to the contrary.

CRT is both the new religion and the indoctrination tool.

Voddie T Baucham Jr claims it promotes a new cosmology:

> *"On the first day, white people created whiteness, a set of normative privileges granted to white-skinned individuals and groups which is "invisible" to those privileged by it";*

> *"On the second day, white people created white privilege, a series of unearned advantages that accrue to white people by virtue of their whiteness;*

> *"On the third day, white people created white supremacy (which is) any belief, behaviour or system that supports, promotes, or enhances white privilege;*

> *"On the fourth day, white people created white complicity, (since) white people, through the practices of whiteness and by benefiting from white privilege, contribute to the maintenance of systemic racial justice;*

> *"On the fifth day, white people created white equilibrium, the belief system that allows white people to*

remain comfortably ignorant;

"On the sixth day, white people created white fragility, the inability and unwillingness of white people to talk about race due to the grip that whiteness, white supremacy, white privilege, white complicity, and white equilibrium exert on them (knowingly or unknowingly)."[xlviii]

A major problem some sections of the conservative think tank have concerning this new religion is that they believe it is only a fad, something so ludicrous that it surely will not endure the test of time.

So, for so many, the matter is so absurd that it does not warrant to be even opposed.

At best, we deploy feeble attempts to oppose it, or as journalist Gemma Tognini wrote in *The Australian* "like Chamberlain, we're attempting to appease monsters".

"When modern tertiary educators are more concerned about making every space "safe" than allowing the contest of ideas to flourish, when demanding something more be done about the outrageous level of domestic abuse among Indigenous women and children in remote parts of Australia is called racist, when a government makes it more affordable for people to take their own lives than increasing funding for palliative care services, when all of this happens and we turn a blind eye, are we any better (than Chamberlain)? What excuse do we have for our collective appeasement?[xlix]

As a matter of fact, not only do we practice collective appeasement, but we also allow ourselves to be indoctrinated by those we feebly attempt to appease.

In the remainder of this chapter, we shall consider the

influence of the media, the influence of the internet, the influence of the school curriculum and universities, the influence of the corporate sector and the influence of the legislative and judiciary arms of government.

Taken each on their own, these various spheres are only influencers. Taken as a group, they become agents of indoctrination.

The undue influence of the media

The media is one of the agencies that pursues an activist agenda in promoting CRT.

It has been accepted for some time now that the media no longer impartially reports news but instead provides a commentary on the news.

The media capacity to provide commentary rather than straight reporting places them in a unique position of promoting a particular worldview among the general population.

A comprehensive research report on the state of the news media in the United States, prepared by the leading multinational Rand Corporation, confirms this.[1]

In their report, Rand reports that in their research they have identified four trends in the United States.

The four trends that Rand has identified and encapsulates under the label of "truth decay" are the following:

1. increasing disagreement about facts and analytical interpretations of facts and data;
2. blurring of the line between opinion and fact;
3. increasing relative volume, and resulting influence, of opinion and personal experience over fact;
4. declining trust in formerly respected sources of factual information.

Opinions are indeed now the main source of news. Gone are the days when news was presented without taking positions. Rand Corporation believes that "media organisations rely on punditry and opinion-based news rather than hard new journalism because the former is relatively inexpensive and allows content to be tailored to specific audiences."

This might be true, but we should not ignore the fact that political correctness strongly influences how the news should be reported. As the saying goes, a picture is worth more than a thousand words and a particular image, a specific camera angle, can carry a message that is misleading because it ignores the wider context.

Advertising also contributes to formulating popular opinion. For instance, the increasing number of advertisements comprising same sex couples has certainly facilitated a vastly different popular view of what a family is.

A common problem we have is that of cognitive bias.

Cognitive bias is the human tendency to accept as truth facts that correspond with our own beliefs and to refuse facts that oppose our own beliefs. So, we isolate ourselves in our thinking by reading only from sources that are partisan to what we stand for. With the wide diversity and large number of media outlets accessible online to most Australians, a number of niches have emerged. These niches cater for particular audiences and particular points of view.

For instance, *The Australian* newspaper is generally regarded as a conservative publication, whilst *The Guardian* gives more support to Labor and Green voters.

By just reading publications that resonate with our beliefs and views, we deprive ourselves of the benefit of hearing "the other side" of the story. We are isolating ourselves, and the more we do so, the more fragile we become in our capacity to accept other points of view.

Also, the more fragile we become, the more self-defensive we become and, therefore, the more we isolate ourselves. This is a vicious circle which then becomes difficult, if not impossible, to break, particularly as the media bombards us with subtle "woke" messages under the veneer of distorted notions of love, fairness and tolerance.

The problem of cognitive bias is accentuated by online media customising what comes on our screens through the use of algorithms.

An algorithm is a set of rules a software program follows to determine a particular outcome.

Algorithms are routinely used in advertising. For instance, it is possible to advertise a particular real estate property for sale on Facebook to an audience that has a specific age profile and geographical location. Algorithms are used to ensure the software limits the advertising of the property to that specific audience.

In this particular instance, the use of the algorithm is inoffensive, however, it can be used to reinforce a particular mindset. For instance, a person who is unusually interested in a particular type of movie will be targeted by being offered programs through his provider of choice (Netflix or other) that satisfy his individual taste.

So, whilst good choices are reinforced, algorithms also reinforce bad choices.

Somebody interested in "feel good" movies will be offered more of the same, but likewise, somebody interested in violent and foul language movies will be also offered more of the same.

Extending this to the news media, messages received on a person's digital device will reinforce the particular political views of the recipient.

Algorithms are used to customise the messages we are exposed to and then reinforce our own cognitive biases.

The result is that we become more entrenched in our positions and viewpoints and less likely to hear anything that contradicts them.

This phenomenon is relatively recent, and it is now exerting an increasing influence on our mindsets.

As remarked in a recent report from the University of Technology, Sydney:

> *"The capacities to personalise and customise news consumption have been made possible by the growth of online news access. In Australia in 2018, news accessed via digital channels surpassed traditional channels, with social media, online news platforms and search engines playing a leading role. As a large and increasing proportion of Australians rely on digital platforms for their news, Australians are increasingly dependent on algorithms 'autonomously' to select the news content they consume. Such algorithms are used both by digital platforms and by traditional news media"* [i].

Most alarmingly, however, is how the Internet media is now undermining parental control.

Until now, most people have accepted the view that parents are the primary parties responsible for the education and nurturing of their children. In that sense, the values of the younger generations are meant to be largely influenced and formed by those imparted by their elders.

However, the Internet is now brainwashing or, if you prefer, indoctrinating our children into particular mindsets.

First of all, it is worth noting that the majority of children nowadays spend an inordinate amount of time online.

A recent report compiled by a leading research institution, the Menzies Centre, reveals that:

> *Children have a particularly difficult time self-*

regulating their screen time use. And there is a large gap
between what parents imagine their children's screen time
to be and what it actually is. A Royal Children's Hospital
Child Health Poll found that parents believe a majority of
Australian kids spend an average of 4.6 hours a weekday
on screens for entertainment, communication and
educational purposes. In reality, the average time for a
teenager is about 6.2 hours a day. More than 21 per cent
of teenagers are spending 12 hours or more on screens on a
typical weekday.[lii]

Naturally, this brings about some physical health issues (for instance, obesity) as well as a lack of ability to engage in face-to-face conversations; it also results in significant psychological problems.

Quoting from the Menzies report again:

"Australians aged between 5 and 24 are now more
likely to be overweight or obese than those of the same age
in the pre-digital era. For example, in 1995, the rates of
obesity of 5–14-year-olds was (sic) 20 per cent and 28 per
cent of 15–24-year-olds. In 2017-18, the proportion of
obese were 24 per cent and 41 per cent respectively.
Adolescents (also) exhibit higher levels of psychological
distress compared to the first decade of this century. For
example, in 2007-08, 6-7 per cent of 18–24-year-old males
reported suffering high or very high psychological distress.
In 2017-18, the same survey conducted by the Australian
Institute of Health and Welfare found that the
proportion in young men had doubled to 12-13 per cent.

Even more alarming is the fact that parents are now powerless to impose controls on the use of their children's Internet.

At the age of 13, a child is now able to disable whatever

parental control devices have been placed on his computer. This is the policy of Google and Apple.

> *"Once your child reaches the age of 13, they will be permitted to maintain their account without participating in family sharing."*
>
> *Apple – Family Privacy Disclosure for Children*[liii]

Immature young minds can therefore be formed by whatever is available through the Internet.

Isolated young persons in the privacy of their bedrooms. Fragile minds lacking discernment. Silent as regards the vital communication exchange that they should engage in with their parents. Silent, fragile and isolated.

So, let us not underestimate the power of social media to influence social opinion.

The Australian newspaper recently reported that whistle blowers have reported that their employer Facebook "banned news in Australia (in 2021) as the Government was considering legislation to force tech giants to pay for news."[liv].

In the process, access was banned to services such as the Department of Fire and Emergency Services, the Council on Homeless Persons, the Australian Medical Association, Suicide Prevention Australia, the Tasmanian Government, SA Health, Fire and Rescue NSW, 1800 Respect and First Nations Media Australia.

A further report also revealed that "Facebook executives deliberately shielded documents showing they wanted to cause havoc to influence media bargaining laws by encouraging staff to falsely label them "attorney-client privileged" despite the files not involving legal issues or being sent to lawyers."[lv]

This clearly proves that the tech giants now have the undoubted capacity to create a world mindset which in turn will have devastating consequences on our capacity to think and debate freely.

Undue influence through education

It would be naïve to believe that critical race theory (CRT) is just a new philosophy debated between university academics and within narrow philosophical and sociological circles.

The reality is that CRT is threatening to infiltrate our Australian schools.

Bella d'Abrera, the director of the Institute of Public Affairs (IPA), one of our leading Australian think tanks, has highlighted the case of Victoria's Parkdale Secondary College, where a visiting social worker labelled boys who were white and Christian as "oppressors" and asked them to stand in front of their peers because of their "privilege".

Also, and, although subsequently acknowledged as "inappropriate" by the school principal, the schoolboys from Brauer College in Warrnambool (Victoria) were told to stand at a school assembly in a symbolic gesture of apology on behalf of their gender.

These are not isolated incidents; this sort of action reflects what is happening overseas, notably in the United States.

Leading sociologist Douglas Murray reports the situation prevailing in Buffalo, Seattle, and California.

In Buffalo, public schools have forced children in kindergarten to watch videos of dead black children to teach them about "police brutality." In California, children in third grade have been taught that they should rank themselves in order of "power" and "privilege", while a new ethnic studies curriculum in the State calls for "counter-genocide" against white Christians. In Seattle, the public schools have claimed that white teachers in the schooling system are "spirit murdering" black children. And then, Douglas Murray adds: "of course, there is always New York. There are case studies enough for a conference in that city alone." [lvi]

However, and as discussed in more detail further on, in Australia, the most significant threat CRT represents is actually embedded in the mindset of the Australian Curriculum Authority (ACARA).

In any event, the matter has been considered to be sufficiently important for the Australian Senate to vote in June 2021 in support of a motion to reject critical race theory from the Australian curriculum.

This issue is also compounded by the fact that, when it comes to academic results, Australian students are continuing to fall behind compared to other leading countries, as well against the results we were achieving a few years ago.

A substantial amount of taxpayer funds has been invested into our Australian schools, starting with Kevin Rudd's computer revolution (every child must have a laptop) and the fact that government reports such as Gonski's have advocated an end to student inequality through the medium of additional expenditure.

This has not worked, and as a result, the Commonwealth government is now looking into how our universities' faculties of education are preparing their future graduates to be "classroom ready".

As far back as 2014, the Teacher Education Ministerial Advisory Group, chaired by Prof. Greg Craven, compiled a report for the Federal Government entitled "Action Now: Classroom Ready Teachers." [lvii]

The key findings of the report were as follows:

"Evidence of poor practice in a number of programs – Not all initial teacher education programs are equipping graduates with the content knowledge, evidence-based teaching strategies and skills

they need to respond to different student learning needs."

"*Insufficient integration of teacher education providers with schools and systems* – Providers, school systems and schools are not effectively working together in the development of new teachers. This is particularly evident in the professional experience component of initial teacher education, which is critical for the translation of theory into practice."

"*Inadequate application of standards* – Initial teacher education providers are not rigorously or consistently assessing the classroom readiness of their pre-service teachers against the Professional Standards."

"*Insufficient professional support for beginning teachers* – Not all graduate teachers are adequately supported once they enter the profession. This means a number of beginning teachers do not reach their full potential, and some may choose to leave the profession."

"*Gaps in crucial information, including workforce data* – Useful information on the effectiveness of initial teacher education and students entering and graduating from initial teacher education is lacking. This hinders both continuous improvement and workforce planning, including the ability to address shortages in specialist subject areas."

The Government endorsed the findings and recommendations of the report, and yet, our performance has continued to deteriorate.

The Programme for International Student Assessment (PISA) is an assessment of student school performance that is conducted every three years in the OECD. The latest published report indicates that students in Australia are now recording their lowest results since this form of international testing began.

After years of decline across various disciplines, Australian students have, for the first time, failed to exceed the OECD average in maths, while also falling in reading and science.

Whilst it is possible that these results are the reflection of a lack of motivation on the part of students (as opined by the State School Teachers of WA Union[lviii]), the issue remains that for some reason (poor teaching standards or failure to motivate students) our education sector is not arousing our younger generations' intellectual curiosity through idea exchanges and debate.

The sheer basics of fundamental knowledge also seem to be lacking for many.

A survey conducted in 2021 by True North Strategy revealed that 84 per cent supported a return to more traditional methods of teaching reading and writing, like phonics; 62 per cent agreed with the proposition that 'politically correct ideological content in the classroom, such as teachers calling Australia Day Invasion Day or promoting the idea that people can choose their gender, is distracting from academic learning and is lowering academic standards', and 69 per cent agreed that academic standards amongst students in Australia are declining relative to other countries[lix]

Ben Jensen, Chief Executive of Australia's leading educational research and consulting group, Learning First, advocates a lesser emphasis on academic research and greater attention to the impact teachers make in the classroom.

In an article published in the *Weekend Australian*[lx], Jensen recommends we focus on "the three factors that most affect student learning in classrooms, what we teach, how we teach, how we assess. He contends that 'the modern policymaker has access to some of the best academic research but has little data on what happens in the classrooms.'"

Apart from the fact that classrooms have now started to be used as a captive audience to a world intent on decrying anything belonging to our past, our students have also been disadvantaged through the pride of place given to inquiry-based learning. Rather than the teacher telling students what they need to know, students are encouraged to explore the material, ask questions, and share ideas.

Inquiry-based learning has its place, but again, it is a matter of balance. It is good to encourage students to be curious, to conduct their own experiments and research, but this assumes, first of all, that the basic foundations have been laid in what used to be called the "3Rs" (reading, writing and arithmetic).

The co-chair of Good to Great Schools Australia, Noel Pearson, reckons that the debate between teacher-directed explicit instruction and inquiry learning has now been running for twice as long as the War of the Roses[lxi] and that it lies at the heart of our schooling problem in Australia.[lxii]

University of NSW Emeritus Professor John Sweller reminds us that "inquiry learning neither teaches us how to inquire nor helps us acquire other knowledge deemed important in the curriculum … (and that) the ultimate evidence against the use of inquiry learning comes from correlational studies based on international tests. Studies such as these asked students to report the extent to which their teachers used inquiry-based learning in their classrooms as opposed to explicit instruction. The results indicated a negative correlation between an emphasis on inquiry learning and international test results." [lxiii]

We have, therefore, an educational problem made up of two components: the growing influence of critical research theory in some Australian schools and the widespread adoption of inquiry-based learning.

The lack of ideological balance stems from both revisions to the Australian school curriculum and the political agitation propagated by student unions. A question mark can also be raised as to whether Australian universities defend freedom of speech.

We will now look in more detail at the impact the school

curriculum and the universities have on our national mindset.

The Australian school curriculum

The Australian school curriculum is a document designed to guide the teaching in all Australian schools from kindergarten to Year 12. The document is compiled by an independent statutory authority: the Australian Curriculum Assessment & Reporting Authority (ACARA).

The recommendations that ACARA makes in the development of the Australian curriculum reflect the guidelines contained in another document known as *The Shape of the Australian Curriculum*. This document, which has been updated over the years, articulates the rationale and goals of our national curriculum.

The Shape of the Australian Curriculum outlines the learning areas of the curriculum (which are largely the subjects being taught) and the dimensions of the curriculum.

The dimensions of the curriculum include creative and critical thinking, personal and social capability, ethical understanding and intercultural understanding.

The Australian curriculum has been the subject of several revisions and has just undergone a significant revision which, initially, created significant concerns in some quarters. The first draft of a very elaborate document, since then fortunately revised and approved, was rejected by the Federal Minister of Education in 2021.

Some of the concerns raised included the following:

- The curriculum reflects a left-wing ideology;
- It denies the positive achievements of the past and labels; the colonisation of Australia as hostile invasion;
- It paints an ungrateful picture of our war heroes;
- It is hostile to Christianity;

- It promotes critical race theory.

To some extent, these concerns were not altogether surprising as they reflected the priorities set in *The Shape of the Australian Curriculum* which are Aboriginal and Torres Strait Islander histories and cultures; Asia and Australia's engagement with Asia; and Sustainability.

The Institute of Public Affairs researched the initial version of the proposed new curriculum in depth and compiled a 111-page submission[lxiv].

It is worthwhile considering some of the pertinent comments they made in this regard

> *"The repeated emphasis on (the priorities set out in The Shape of the Australian Curriculum) throughout the Foundation to Year 10 English curriculum means that other important aspects of 'English' are omitted. The only European literature mentioned in the Foundation to Year 10 curriculum, for example, appears to be Cinderella and Jack and the Beanstalk. While there are frequent references to the Dreamtime and Asian literature, there is no mention at all of texts that have been foundational to western and therefore Australian literature – for example, Homer, Virgil, the Bible, Chaucer, Shakespeare, and Milton, among many others which could have warranted a mention."*

> *"Year 7 students who formerly learned "How Australia is a secular nation and a multi-faith society with a Christian heritage (ACHCK051)" will now be told that "Australia is a culturally diverse, multifaith, secular and pluralistic society with diverse communities, such as the distinct communities of First Nations Australians (AC9HC7K05)".*

> *"Year 8 students who used to be taught about "[t]he*

values and beliefs of religions practised in contemporary Australia, including Christianity (ACHCK065) will now study "how groups express their particular identities, including national identity, and how this influences active citizenship, belonging and perceptions of their citizenship, including First Nations People of Australia, religious, cultural and/or community groups (AC9HC8K06)".

The Federal Government of the day (through the Minister of Education of the Morrison Government), claiming to take heed of some of these concerns, ordered a complete review of the proposed curriculum. Unfortunately, and although some minor improvements were achieved, the final version (adopted by all Australian States) still reveals significant political and indoctrination bias.

Furthermore, even the teaching profession itself has significant reservations: the media recently reported that the Australian Primary Principals Association is concerned about overcrowding and the impossibility of teaching the required content if taken literally.

This proves the point that we are in the middle of a culture war which could jeopardise our ability to think individually, creatively and fairly and confine us, instead, into a mould of narrow-minded, negative, pessimistic thinking, offering no solutions to our so-called "race issue" predicament.

Before closing this section on schools and school curricula, it would be very remiss of me not to mention the impact of a number of organisations that receive government funding. These promote a view that disempowers parents and guardians from having the last say on how their children should be educated. I raised this issue briefly in Chapter 2, but, as it is so vital to the future of free speech and democracy, I feel the need to refer to it again here.

The best known of these government-funded organisations, of course, is the Safe Schools Coalition. This was funded by the Federal Government for a few years on the understanding that the purpose of the coalition was to protect children from bullying. However, funding has since stopped since the programme really had nothing to do with bullying but rather with promoting the LGBTQI lifestyle in Australian schools.

Unfortunately, since then, the program has been transferred into the hands of other organisations which, under the guise of a broader agenda (such as mental health, student well-being and youth assistance), promote the same ideology enabled by the financial assistance they receive from a number of government departments. To name just two, for instance; the Student Well Being Hub/Australian Well Being Framework is funded by the Australian Department of Education; whilst Headspace National Youth Mental Foundation is funded by the Australian Department of Health.

Both support the damaging woke ideology of gender being a social construct rather than a biological reality.

It, therefore, turns out that the challenge with education in Australia is not what government and private schools teach daily, Mondays to Fridays, but the myriad of other information available through specialised hubs, channels and organisations that benefit from taxpayer financial support. It is often online, more discreet and less visible, almost clandestine than what is taught in classrooms, but it is very influential, particularly in the hands of educators who espouse the woke movement.

The student unions at the universities

Australian student unions exercise a significant amount of control over what is debated at universities. In the main, they represent left-wing, anti-bourgeois/conservative organisations and the first taste of university life of any new student on campus.

Leading Australian columnist Janet Albrechtsen believes the problem is the lack of control exercised by vice-chancellors.

In an article entitled *O-Week censors excel themselves*[lxv], she writes:

> *"How much longer can university leaders ignore the accelerating rhythm to raids on free speech at Australian universities? Today, the most brazen opponents of free speech within universities are those who control student unions. Funded by other students' money, the leaders of student unions use their union muscle to control what other students hear, read and learn."*

Albrechtsen cites the case of the student union at Monash University, which runs Orientation Week stalls and other events to new students. She explains how this union rejected a booking application from Generation Liberty, an offshoot of the conservative think tank, the Australian Institute of Public Affairs (IPA) on the grounds that the Institute's views on climate change do not align with those of the Monash University Student Association.

Now, irrespective of the position one holds on climate change, the issue at stake surely is that all viewpoints should be encouraged to be expressed on a university campus in an attempt to clarify thinking, debunk myths and find true knowledge.

This should particularly be the case with Monash University, as the Victorian Equal Opportunity Act 2010 (in line with similar legislation in other states) does not allow discrimination on the grounds of political beliefs or activities.

University vice-chancellors will, of course, deny that these incidents reflect the ethos of their university, but the reality is they do very little to prevent them from occurring.

As Lt-Gen David Morrison said in August 2021: "The standard you walk past is the standard you accept."

In 2019, the IPA carried out a survey that gave the following results[lxvi]:

- 41% of students feel they are sometimes unable to express their opinion at university;
- 31% of students have been made to feel uncomfortable by a university teacher for expressing their opinion;
- 47% of students feel more comfortable expressing their views on social media than at university;
- 59% of students believe they are sometimes prevented from voicing their opinions on controversial issues by other students.

The survey was of students of all political persuasions – 39% of students supported the ALP, 28% supported the Greens, 14% supported the Coalition, 20% were Other and Undecided.

This is despite the current educational standards applicable to all higher education providers.

The issue of free speech on campus has now been brought to the attention of our legislators, thanks to what is commonly referred to as the "French Report".

In 2019, at the request of Hon Dan Tehan MP, the Federal Minister for Education, the Hon. Robert French published the Report of the Independent Review of Freedom of Speech in Australian Higher Education Providers.[lxvii]

The Report recommended some changes to the existing legislative standards binding the universities. It also recommended the introduction of a model code of conduct.

The recommendation to introduce a **voluntary** (my emphasis) code of conduct was based on the premise that any code would have the following objects:

(1) To ensure that the freedom of lawful speech of staff and students at the university and visitors to the university is treated as a paramount value and therefore is not restricted nor its exercise unnecessarily burdened by restrictions or burdens other than those imposed by law and set out in the Principles of the Code;

(2) To ensure that academic freedom is treated as a defining value by the university and therefore not restricted nor its exercise unnecessarily burdened by restrictions or burdens other than those imposed by law and set out in the Principles of the Code;

(3) To affirm the importance of the university's institutional autonomy under law in the regulation of its affairs, including in the protection of freedom of speech and academic freedom.

The report also recommended that the Code be applied to:

(1) the governing body of the university, its officers and employees and its decision-making organs, including those involved in academic governance and to

(2) student representative bodies to the extent that they have policies and rules which are capable of being applied to restrict or burden the freedom of speech of anyone, or academic freedom.

Meanwhile, the jury is still out as to whether a growing number of universities will see fit to adopt a voluntary code of conduct along the lines suggested by Justice Robert French.

The influence of the corporate sector

The influence of the corporate sector ("big business") on the mindset of the average Australian is considerable.

The leading top corporate individuals, the billionaires of this world, carry significant influence and power over society and governments. Their considerable individual wealth allows them to exercise a degree of control of society that is, honestly, very concerning.

The leading world financial intelligence agency, Wealth X, reported that there were 295,450 ultra-wealthy individuals in the world in 2021, with a combined total net worth of $35.5 trillion US dollars (a trillion dollars is one million million dollars).

It is greatly concerning to see that the majority of these ultra-wealthy individuals have now embraced the cause of wokeism, as another way of promoting their business.

Businesses nowadays promote their goods and services by espousing current cultural trends to make themselves more appealing to the rising new progressive generation of consumers and decision-makers.

In turn, this influences the mindset and opinions of the general population.

By virtue of its wealth, the corporate world also exercises a significant degree of influence over our duly elected representatives and therefore weakens the power of the democratic vote, which is the cornerstone of the freedom of expression and belief.

Leading Australian academic, Carl Rhodes, denounces the misused power of this corporate mindset in his book *"Woke Capitalism, how corporate morality is sabotaging democracy."*[lxviii].

In his work, Rhodes brings our attention to a report prepared by the World Inequality Lab, pointing out that income inequality has increased in nearly all countries.

Rhodes believes that the very large multinational corporations are becoming concerned, in view of this state of affairs, that the political tide might be starting to turn against them and that, ultimately, their economic status might be compromised.

Rhodes believes that many CEOs have become woke activists in an effort to appease the growing popular concern presented by the lack of economic equality.

Rhodes is of the opinion that corporate wokeism is a self-defence mechanism initiated by the economic powerful in order to retain the political and economic advantage.

His view is that the great majority of the larger corporates are not interested in altruism but simply in preserving their status quo by way of virtue-signalling.

Be it as it may, the point is that, with an increasing focus on wokeism, the multi nationals are clearly influencing the mindset of the general population, not only through their own recruitment policies and business practices, but through their substantial donations and their public advertising.

Rhodes' book includes a plethora of examples of corporate leaders making substantial donations to particular causes. Among those, Jeff Bezos, founder of Amazon, is reported to have made a $10 billion commitment to "develop ways to protect the natural world"; Warren Buffet gives billions towards the social justice woke cause, and in 2019 Michael Bloomberg pledged half a billion dollars towards closing down coal-powered electricity plants.

Well-known corporate names that have embraced the woke agenda include such likes as Qantas, Telstra, Commonwealth Bank, AGL Energy, NRMA insurance, Amazon, Gillette, Ben & Jerry, Adidas, Coca-Cola, Medibank, Netflix, as well as a plethora of others.

Recently, it was reported that the BBC promised that by 2027 a quarter of its staff will be recruited from working-class backgrounds (presumably, irrespective of merit).[lxix].

Also, as reported by Douglas Murray in his excellent work *The War on the West*, employees at Cigna, one of America's largest health insurance providers, have likewise been routinely subjected to CRT lessons. These have included them being lectured on "white privilege", "gender privilege", and "religious privilege", and being advised not to consider white men in hiring decisions. And at one of America's most successful companies, Coca-Cola, employees have been made to go through "anti-racism" training that aimed to teach workers how to "be less white."[lxx]

Living in an extremely visual society with television, social media, and a significant amount of imagery being screened every day on our phones and tablets, all portraying the same type of message, the risk of indoctrination to a particular worldview becomes highly significant.

The influence of the legislature

In Australia, we hold to the Westminster system of government which essentially divides the functions of government into three different branches: the executive, the legislative and the judiciary.

The executive (the government) recommends new laws to the legislative (parliament), and laws passed by parliament are then applied and enforced by the judiciary (the courts). This illustrates the principle of the Separation of Powers.

This system is meant to uphold our democracy. We elect our government; we elect our members of parliament, and we accept that the courts will apply the laws passed by those that we have duly elected.

Most people would consider our Australian system of

government as good democracy, but one should note that the parliamentary democratic process is significantly hindered in the Australian Parliament by the tight control exercised by party "power brokers" in the recruitment of candidates. This is particularly the case for the Australian Labor Party, where the trade unions play a significant role, resulting in a party faction system that does not necessarily represent the views of the rank-and-file voters.

The importance of party discipline cannot be underestimated either, and it is common knowledge that any Labor member of parliament who decides to "cross the floor" to vote for the other side will lose his or her chances of party preselection at the next election. The saying goes, "Cross the floor and out the door!"

To that extent, freedom of expression is curtailed in the political process in Australia.

Furthermore, there is no real discussion between the parties about particular bills. Any discussion that takes place is a matter of negotiation of what the other party would be prepared to offer in exchange for partial support of a particular bill.

In this sense, the system is one where the parties isolate themselves in their own echo chambers, shutting their ears as to the merits of any particular bill introduced in the House. Basically, the Government proposes and the Opposition always (or nearly always) opposes. There is no dialogue, and therefore, nobody listens to anything other than the sound of their own voice or the sound of their party's voice.

This is not really democratic, but the major parties have a vested interest in not changing this system, which explains why there has been no effort made to adopt or adapt any of the various other models of government that have been tried elsewhere, such as for instance the Citizens' Referenda in Switzerland or the D'Hondt method,[lxxi] where (in the case of the latter), after all votes have been cast, succeeding quotients are calculated for each party.[8]

I acknowledge that the merits of these other systems are outside the scope of this book, but it is nevertheless important to make the point that in the Australian context (which is the only scope of this book), some improvements in our election system could be considered to achieve a better democratic outcome and support freedom of expression and belief.

The influence of the judiciary

Turning now to the role of the courts in the democratic process, we note that over the years, there has been a tendency for them to take gradual control of the legislative process.

In 2015, Monash University Professor Jeffrey Goldsworthy already sounded the alarm in an article published in the Quadrant journal titled *Losing Faith in Democracy, why judicial supremacy and activism is rising and what to do about it.*

In that article, he mentions that the problem is not confined to Australia or the United Kingdom. He reminds us that in 1939, only a handful of countries had a judicial review of their constitution, but by 2011, the number had grown to 83 per cent.

He explains that the new rights culture prevailing worldwide has facilitated the process.

It is no wonder, therefore, that Australia has not been spared in this regard.

International human rights legislation has also played a major role in the process, and Goldsworthy argues that these developments "amount to a constitutional experiment on a global scale; they raise the danger of democratic decision-making being subject to override not only by local judges but by

---

[8] In the D'Hondt system, the party with the largest quotient wins one seat and the quotient is recalculated. The process is repeated until the required number of seats is filled.

reference to a global judicial consensus about rights".

Courts are now expected to interpret legislation to ensure that they are consistent with protected international rights. Although there is much merit in this, the problem is that the sovereignty of the democratic parliamentary process is diminished.

It is really now up to the High Court "experts" to decide whether the duly elected Australian Parliament is entitled to pass a particular piece of legislation.

Of course, I am not trying to argue that the Australian Parliament always has it "right", but the difference is that the composition of the Australian Parliament can be changed by popular vote, but not so the composition of the High Court.

High Court judges in Australia are appointed by the Governor-General, having been selected by Cabinet on the advice of the Attorney-General. Effectively then, Cabinet makes the choice.

The choice of the appointment can therefore be easily influenced by the particular ideology of the government in office at the time.

Of course, in a perfect world, this should not matter as judges would then interpret the Australian Constitution through impartial eyes rather than let their own ideologies influence their judgment.

Yet, this is not always the case, and the problem arises in particular when High Court judges start looking into the issue of "implied rights" when deciding whether a particular piece of legislation, passed by Parliament, is actually valid under the Australian Constitution.

What are implied rights? They are rights that judges believe exist implicitly in the Australian Constitution, although they are not expressly stated in so many words in the document itself.

Implied rights are usually referred to in the context of Governments being prevented by the courts from passing particular laws because these laws are considered, in the eyes of the courts, in breach of specific human rights implied in our Australian Constitution.

One could argue that if the Australian constitution were more up-to-date with human rights, the courts would not have to look for the possible existence of any implied ones.

However, this viewpoint is naive because it is very difficult in practice to carry out any changes to the Australian Constitution. Very few attempts made to amend our Constitution have ever been successful, as by law, any constitutional changes are required to be passed by a majority of voters in a majority of the Australian states.

The problem we are left with is this: as the courts start upholding certain rights they perceive to be breached by parliamentary legislation, we are in a position where public debate becomes stifled.

When a government enacts laws that are considered unjust or oppressive by a majority of the population, our democratic system allows us to remove this particular government from office at the next election and vote for a party that will revoke such legislation. However, when a court makes a particular pronouncement that might sound unfair to a majority of the people, the court's judgement cannot be reversed. Judges are not elected. They are appointed. They are meant to be impartial, but this does not mean, in any way, that their judgements will be popular.

Furthermore, judgements passed by the High Court tend to be technical and, therefore, out of the grasp of the general understanding of the majority of the Australian population.

The real problem with judicial activism is that it assumes High Court judges have a supervisory role over the Australian Constitution. They decide whether the meaning of the words adopted in the original document (as well as in the few successive amendments made to it) is still fair in the present Australian context in the 21st century. They become part of an elite group of experts who know better than we do what is good for us.

To illustrate the extent to which the High Court is sometimes prepared to go to override legislation that it does not endorse, we can mention the case of Turkish-born Delil Alexander, who had his Australian citizenship cancelled in 2021 following a finding by our Australia national security agency, ASIO, that he had joined a terrorist organisation.

Although the Minister at the time had relied on the discretionary powers conferred to him under the Citizenship Act and claimed that Alexander had repudiated his allegiance to Australia, the High Court disagreed.

The High Court effectively overruled the validity of the legislation, claiming that it was punitive and that it deprived the plaintiff from his human rights to live at liberty in Australia.

The Minister's decision was revoked by the High Court.

Similarly, in 2020, in the case of Love vs Commonwealth, two overseas individuals who had committed serious crimes in Australia were allowed by the High Court to stay, on the grounds of their Aboriginal descent, which in the eyes of the Court protected them from deportation to their respective countries of birth.

In the search for solutions to the growing problem of judicial activism, it has been suggested that enacting a Bill of Rights would provide better guidance to the judiciary and protect it from ideological bias.

Unfortunately, this is incorrect.

Political rights are not absolute rights.

As Professor Goldsworthy reminds us in the journal article cited above, even the right to life is not absolute, as it can be overridden in self-defence. The right to free speech is also subject to many limitations, national security, privacy etc. It is also impossible to decide in advance how human rights, stated in an abstract form, should be weighed against competing rights and interests.

It is beyond the scope of this book to analyse in which particular instances a judicial review of our Australian Constitution has proved to be beneficial to our society. Suffice to say at this juncture, the increasing prevalence of this relatively new culture of "rights" in Australia provides dangerous ammunition for an unelected judiciary to take precedence over the will of the people, expressed in our parliaments.

Summary

Woke ideology has been painted in attractive terms through the use of positive emotions grounded in a new definition of love and tolerance. Critical Race Theory (CRT), which is at the base of the woke ideology, is now being elevated to religious status.

CRT is promoted through significant spheres of influence which contribute to forming a particular mindset. In this regard, the media holds pride of place as it focuses more on the provision of commentary than actual factual reporting.

The media are also in a position to exploit human cognitive bias through the use of algorithms that ensure the news we receive corresponds to our own core beliefs and prejudices. This has been particularly facilitated through the explosion of social media channels and the lack of parental control over children's use of the Internet.

Incidents have occurred in schools (although more frequently in the United States) that testify to a deliberate intent of promoting woke ideology as a new attractive philosophy.

A revision of the Australian curriculum has been challenged by the Minister for Education in the former Morrison government. The Australian Senate found it appropriate to endorse a motion rejecting CRT from the Australian curriculum.

Our capacity to think properly as a nation is under threat, as evidence indicates that our universities do not prepare our future teachers as well as they should. International comparisons also show that Australian students are falling behind their overseas counterparts.

Australian universities do not tolerate academic staff who challenge CRT, and student unions are particularly adept at preventing the promotion of anything that opposes woke ideology on campus.

The top corporate sector has now identified that the promotion of woke ideology could become a lucrative marketing ploy to improve their own bottom line.

Our parliamentary system is not well equipped to facilitate the engagement of proper debate, and the courts have resorted for some time to interpreting our laws, particularly our Australian Constitution, in the light of the particular beliefs and aspirations of some of those sitting in judgement.

As a whole, the cumulative influence of the media, educational, legislative, judicial and business sector constitute a formidable and dangerous force to be reckoned with by our democracy.

Chapter 8

Tolerance, Acceptance, Justice

They might claim to pursue true justice but all seek only favourable treatment.

Throughout this book, I made it clear that, nowadays, the main charge levied against our society is that of racism.

Woke persons believe that the West is fundamentally racist, and since Australia is largely made up of Western European immigrants, Australian society is accused of being racist.

The question is whether there is any grain of truth in this and, if so, what can be done about it.

The other follow-up question that also needs to be raised is whether Australia was ever a tolerant society, for racism only occurs in an intolerant context. Without intolerance, there could not be racism.

Much has been written already on the subject of intolerance.

According to Herbert Marcuse, true tolerance assumes "intolerance toward prevailing policies, attitudes, opinions, and the extension of tolerance to policies, attitudes, and opinions which are outlawed or suppressed."[lxxii]

The American philosopher Herbert Marcuse was one of the key players in the radical Left Frankfurt School in the 1960s. His impact on the youth movement of the 60s was considerable.

Marcuse really believed that true tolerance should be granted to the Left (in his mind, the side of the oppressed) and denied to the Right (in his mind, the side of the oppressor). He thought that unless intolerance of the Right was practised, true tolerance (i.e., tolerance for the ideas of the Left) would never be "liberated".

Not too surprisingly, this is very much what wokeism preaches. Intolerance towards the speech, writings and accomplishments of the heterosexual white European and "freedom" for the non-white or non-binary or non-European individual.

So wokeism fails its apparent aim of tolerance because, although it claims to pursue an agenda of tolerance, it actually uses the tools of intolerance to promote its cause.

Full acceptance is now the new intolerance. The New Left shall not tolerate anything other than full acceptance of its agenda.

For instance, whilst the LGBTQI+ movement has now won the marriage referendum in Australia and obtained a change to the definition of marriage in the Marriage Act, this accomplishment is no longer considered enough.

The LGBTQI+ movement now demands that the Australian population fully embraces its lifestyle, not just tolerate it, but promote it and endorse all the values it represents.

This is why the battle for religious freedom in Australia is so intense.

In early 2022, the Morrison government tried to protect the religious freedom of religious schools in Australia, but facing assured defeat in the Senate, it then decided to withdraw its own Bill from the Notice Paper.

Indeed, if the amendments passed in the House of Representatives had been supported in the Senate, the original intent of the legislation would have been totally lost.

Instead of protecting the religious freedom of the religious schools, these schools would have faced the burden of unconditionally enrolling students who defy the binary scientific concept of gender. In other words, all religious schools would have been expected to fully embrace the transgender agenda. To support it without passing judgement, without any conditions.

To win this battle, the woke movement had no hesitation in misrepresenting what the legislation really stood for.

This is standard tactics. Basically, the message is: I don't want to hear you, but I don't want anyone else to hear you either, and I will do my utmost to ensure that if they hear you, they do not really hear what you say, but instead hear my misrepresentation of your argument … lest they agree with you.

The Australian social policy think tank *The Institute for Civil Society* recently posted an analysis of the five biggest objections to the Religious Discrimination Bill.

Quoting from their website.[lxxiii]:

> *Objection 1: The Religious Discrimination Bill is unnecessary.*
>
> *Answer from the Institute: Incorrect. Discrimination against people of faith is legal in NSW and SA; the ECAJ 2020 antisemitism report and the Islamophobia Report 2019 also document many cases of religious discrimination.*
>
> *Objection 2: The Religious Discrimination Bill allows religious schools to fire gay teachers or expel gay students.*
>
> *Answer from the Institute: Incorrect. The Bill does not affect the federal Sex Discrimination Act 1984 protecting teachers or students from discriminatory actions.*
>
> *Objection 3: The Religious Discrimination Bill will legalise hate speech.*

Answer from the Institute: Incorrect. The Bill will protect statements of belief (or unbelief) which are made in good faith, not malicious, harassing, threatening, intimidating or vilifying.

Objection 4: The Religious Discrimination Bill will threaten health care for minorities.

Answer from the Institute: Incorrect. The RDB does not provide any right or protection to a medical professional to discriminate against their(sic) patients in type or quality of medical care.

Objection 5: The Religious Discrimination Bill will wind back protections for women, disabled and LGBTQI+.

Answer from the Institute: The Bill only relates to discrimination on the grounds of religious belief or activity. It does not authorise discrimination on the grounds of any other protected attributes, such as race, sex, sexual orientation, gender identity or disability and it does not change the protection against discriminatory acts based on those protected attributes under any other laws.

The Institute for Civil Society is a reputable organisation. Its website states that its objectives are as follows:

1. Promote recognition and respect for the institutions of civil society that exist between individuals and the government. Included in this space are clubs, schools, religious organisations, charities and NGOs.

2. Uphold traditional rights and liberties, including the freedoms of association, expression, conscience and religion.

3. Promote a sensible and civil discussion about how to balance competing rights and freedoms in Australian society.

The Institute for Civil Society is staffed by legally qualified academics.

Mark Sneddon was formerly Associate Professor of Law at the University of Melbourne Law School;

Dr Sharon Rodrick holds a BA, LLB (Hons) (Melb), LLM (Melb), PhD (Monash).and has worked as a teaching and research academic for over twenty-five years, specialising in media law, freedom of the media and property law. She has co-authored a textbook in media law and is published on privacy law, open justice and restrictions on journalists and reporting.

Dr Simon Kennedy is a Research Analyst at the Institute for Civil Society. His work at the ICS involves researching and writing on state and federal policy regarding freedom of conscience, freedom of speech, and freedom of religion.

We can rest assured that these academics understand how to read acts of parliament.

We can be confident that their opinion is professionally well-researched.

Now, in case, you, the reader, accept this but still think that those who objected to the Religious Discrimination Bill might have been well-intentioned but unfortunately ignorant, I should clarify that all of the above objections were made by well-educated people: journalists, radio presenters and senior officials who, I presume, have easy access to professional lawyers and other legal analysts who can provide, if required, an impartial opinion of the legislation in question.

My point is that the opposition to free speech is now so strong that some will not hesitate to misrepresent the true intent of any proposed legislation if it serves the purpose of achieving full acceptance of their views – full acceptance obtained by full enforcement.

This is not only highly objectionable behaviour, but it also shows absolute contempt and disrespect of one's adversary. It is really the beginning of the end of democracy, the demise of free speech. It is totalitarian.

How do we get out of this horrible predicament?

We need to start tolerating each other's opinions.

Tolerance of opinion presumes respect for freedom of expression.

I am not sure how we can regain this form of respect.

It would, of course, presume that we can first listen to each other patiently; listen without interrupting; listen with the aim of understanding; listen with the aim of discovering the truth; of testing one's opinions.

This is the complete antithesis to the current "if you do not agree with me, you must hate me, so there is no need for me to listen to you."

In other words, I do not have to tolerate you because you are not prepared to fully embrace my viewpoint.

We do not respect each other anymore because we have fallen into the trap of believing that we can only respect persons who have the same opinion as ours.

By doing so, we exalt ourselves. We actually make ourselves morally superior to all those who have different views. We think we are the guardians of all that is good, all that is valuable, and although we claim to oppose racism, we actually promote it by considering anyone inferior who happens to harbour a different view from ours.

In the second decade of the 21st century, the woke movement believes it is the new moral compass our society needs.

Unless the woke movement adopts a humbler and more reasonable approach, the possibility of sustaining a meaningful intellectual dialogue does not exist.

The woke movement needs to change, but the rest of society also needs to change.

We who are not woke need to overcome the fear that I discussed in an earlier chapter of this book – the fear of being shut down, the fear of losing our employment, the fear of losing friends.

We are in a battle, and nobody can ever go into a battle paralysed with fear.

We need to foster the opportunity for calm and unemotional debate instead of always defaulting to a classic avoidance strategy, which only brings isolation and the demise of intellectual thought.

We also need to regain a sense of what true justice is.

If we are honest with ourselves, we must admit that many of us do not seek true justice but only favourable treatment.

The current means of seeking favourable treatment consist in seeking equality of outcome.

Early classical 19th-century liberalism philosophy called for equality before the law, not equality of outcome. In other words, retributive justice, not distributive justice.

Retributive justice is based on the principle that you receive what you deserve. In other words, penalties and trophies reflect your achievements. Distributive justice, on the other hand, claims that what you deserve is not based on your achievements; what you deserve is just the same treatment as everyone else. In other words, I cannot be favoured any less than anyone else.

This is because under distributive justice, there is no meritocracy. It does not matter what your efforts have been, you receive the same share as everyone else.

Distributive justice assumes that merits are not equally distributed because already, at the starting line, there is no level playing field. Some are rich; some are poor; some are gifted;

some are not; some are born lazy; others are endowed with a hard-working temperament.

The so-called merits then accrue more easily to those who are favoured by their backgrounds, education or temperament and therefore, it would be unfair to favour them even further in the administration of justice.

They should really get the same outcome, the same treatment, the same share as all the others.

This is actually the heart of woke philosophy.

According to distributive justice, all are meant to receive the same outcome, but because in the past this has not happened, we now redress the balance or overcompensate by only providing justice to those deemed to have missed out or who are now considered "unprivileged" by accident of birth, environment or some other factor.

Allowing the so-called privileged class to have a say in the current debate of ideas about what type of society we want would be unfair. According to the woke movement, these people have already had their "say". They have already made their contributions in centuries past. It is now the turn of the Other to speak up.

What is the result of this state of affairs? Simply a series of monologues. The white heterosexual middle-class, middle-aged European made his monologue in the past, so it is considered that justice is now served only if the opportunity of the next monologue is extended, exclusively, to the so-called "oppressed."

Therefore, we both live in our own echo chambers and become more and more isolated from each other.

Summary

Although it might be true that Australia has never been a fully tolerant society, if indeed it is possible for such a society to exist, in its struggle to combat intolerance, wokeism advocates a different approach. It preaches something more akin to what Herbert Marcuse advocated: the total intolerance of everything currently tolerated.

This new type of intolerance demands full acceptance of what has not been tolerated in the past.

One of its main targets is religious freedom. This explains why the Scott Morrison Government Religious Freedom Bill did not pass beyond the House of Representatives.

In its quest to impose by force a full acceptance of its agenda, the woke movement promotes distributive justice.

Whereas traditionally retribution was at the core of our justice philosophy (people were rewarded for positive outcomes and punished for negative ones), the postmodern concept of justice entails a distribution model of equal shares to all, irrespective of merits.

This approach had already been advocated as an economic model by Karl Marx in the 19th century, but it is now extended to non-economic issues, with a fundamental focus on the new definition of racism.

In particular, the new tolerance philosophy no longer tolerates the voice of the conservative white male. Its view of justice demands that the right to speak be exclusively granted to the so-called oppressed classes.

Misrepresentation is an acceptable weapon that can be used, if necessary, in this new quest for the conquest of our society.

Instead of facilitating respectful and intelligent dialogue, postmodernism misrepresents or shuts down its opponents and advocates a new type of monologue: the New Atheist Left has the floor.

Chapter 9

What About Multiculturalism?

"The deal with multiculturalism is that the only culture you are allowed to disapprove of is your own."

(Martin Amis)

According to Encyclopedia Britannica, **multiculturalism** is "the view that cultures, races, and ethnicities, particularly those of minority groups, deserve special acknowledgment of their differences within a dominant political culture".

At first glance, multiculturalism appears to be a compassionate, broadminded, tolerant practice that accepts the different Other.

Unfortunately, far from being compassionate and loving, multiculturalism has isolated communities and provided no encouragement to assimilate into the dominant culture.

Naturally, this is not the official view in Australia.

The Australian Human Rights Commission sings the praises of multiculturalism.

In a speech to the Sydney Institute in March 2016[9], the Australian Human Rights Commissioner declared that multiculturalism has been good for our country and that, whilst in the case of Europe, migrant communities have found it

---

[9] https://humanrights.gov.au/about/news/speeches/success-australias-multiculturalism, accessed 18/11/2022

difficult to assimilate, the situation in Australia is not the same.

In that speech, the Commissioner went on to say that "on social cohesion, even multiculturalism's critics would readily concede the social miracle of Australia's twentieth and twenty-first-century migration history."

This might be superficially true: for instance, many children of immigrants have embraced the Australian way of life, its sports, foods, and social practices. Second generations of immigrants usually speak English well and often achieve great academic success. In my case, I have perfectly blended into the Australian culture and even engaged in Australian political activism. My three children are, above all, Australian citizens.

However, a deeper analysis of multiculturalism will reveal that it has failed Australia.

In case I might be misunderstood, I should hasten to say that I have no objection to the fact that Australia, long ago, abolished its "white only" immigration policy.

I do not discriminate on the grounds of colour.

My objection to multiculturalism is somewhat different.

Multiculturalism in Australia has failed us on a number of fronts.

Firstly, it has failed us in handling the issues concerning the Aboriginal and Torres Straits population.

Our Australian brand of multiculturalism has limited itself to much virtue signalling, such as paying homage to the traditional inhabitants of the land on which we stand, or pronouncing official "sorry statements" and, more recently, in discussing the merits of an official Voice in the Australian Parliament.

Such practices have done nothing to address the difficult conditions under which most of the Aboriginal population live; done nothing to eradicate the violence perpetrated in remote communities, the abuse of drugs and alcohol.

Much money has been spent, countless administrative bodies

have been formed, but the day-to-day living conditions have not changed.

Secondly, multiculturalism has fuelled the current crisis of identity politics.

Rather than upholding a well-defined set of national values, multiculturalism fosters group identities and group values.

The problem with this is that group values vary from one group to another, particularly due to the issue of intersectionality, which I discuss in Chapter 1.

For instance, according to Critical Race Theory, the values of a white homosexual will vary with those of a black homosexual and, whilst the values of the LGBTQI movement have already clashed with those of the transgender activists, the values of the feminist movement are confrontational to the male into female sport lobby.

In a recent article in the newspaper *The Spectator*, leading writer and social commentator Dave Pellow denounces the nonsense of multiculturalism:

> *"Multiculturalism means we should invite the fabric of our national identity to be woven with more and more random threads until the pattern and design of a nation is unrecognisable. Nations lose their identity and its people lose their heritage. Multicultural is to dilute that which makes us who we are by the grace of God until the remaining flavour is bland and indistinct."*[lxxiv]

Multiculturalism will praise the virtues of diversity, but diversity without cohesion, unfortunately, leads us to a diversity of aggression.

In Australia, we use multiculturalism as a tool for self-penitence, a constant reminder that we have failed and that we do not really know how to live harmoniously with each other.

A more positive approach is required to find our way out of

our present sociological predicament. This will need dialogue, not a dialogue between the elites of the Left and Right but a dialogue with our neighbours, our friends and our family members.

This dialogue can only be fruitful if we manage to frame a common set of values, a morality that binds us.

We cannot expect our governments to show the lead in this regard.

Indeed, successive governments in this country and abroad have been very adept at promoting multiculturalism to satisfy the needs of new generations of "psychological" men and women, self-centred on their own needs and aspirations.

They do this to maximise the votes they receive in their favour. Yet, an appeal to the emotions of the populace is not always the same as acting in the best interests of those who vote for you.

Furthermore, governments claim to be neutral when it comes to religion and individual beliefs and scramble to try to satisfy everyone, whilst in the process satisfying none or few indeed.

Rather than promoting multiculturalism, our efforts should be focused on determining the values that bind us as a nation with words that everyone can understand and relate to – not the liberty, equality and fraternity of the French Republic. These word concepts are too broad, with too many nuances of meaning; they are meant to unify, but they do not, as too many interpret them differently.

Rather than indulging in a current virtue-signalling brand of multiculturalism, we should perhaps revisit the practices of respecting the Other, listening to the Other, desiring to learn from the Other, asking the Other how we can help and learning again to agree to disagree.

Some call this interculturalism. I think this is a big word for ideas and practices that were considered just good manners and basic morals in different times.

In an excellent article on the subject, Professor Augusto Zimmerman quoted a retired professor of politics at Oxford University, John Gray, for saying that a truly democratic society "cannot be radically multicultural but depends for its successful renewal across the generations on an undergirding culture that is held in common.[lxxv]

Many in Australia want to continue to live in a democratic society but, unfortunately, fail to appreciate that this cannot happen unless we agree on the fundamentals.

In the past, these fundamentals in Australia were known as hard work, fair go, and mateship. These unifying concepts are now becoming old-fashioned and have been replaced by a vague mixed bag of fake moral values, inimical to freedom of speech and belief.

It is high time to reverse this dangerous trajectory.

Summary

Multiculturalism is a wolf in sheep's clothing. It comes across as being broadminded, tolerant and compassionate, but on a deeper analysis, it proves to be divisive as it promotes identity politics.

Official bodies such as the Australian Human Rights Commission claim that Australia has achieved unparalleled success with multiculturalism, but this analysis is superficial: it ignores the fact that much of what used to be has now been replaced by ill-defined values that vie against each for supremacy and continue to erode our fundamental rights to freedom of speech and belief.

Chapter 10

Conclusion

As I mentioned in the introductory chapter, the decision to write this book has been motivated by a concern for the new generations and generations yet to come.

I have identified to the best of my ability some of the distant (and not so distant!) causes of the unfortunate state of affairs that prevails in Australia.

I have tried to show that there are significant areas of influence at work that manipulate the mindsets of our Australian population.

Discussion is no longer welcome, and anything that might jeopardise the power of the corporate world and the tech giants is forcefully opposed and, if need be, ridiculed.

Misrepresentations of historical events and vilifications of laws ostensibly intended for the good of our country are now rife.

I do not presume to have a magic solution to a complex sociological problem that transcends the boundaries of our nation and affects many other Western-culture civilisations.

Nevertheless, I think it would be remiss of me to write a book just to deplore our current state of affairs so I will offer some tentative remedies in five broad areas:

- Legislation
- Education
- Religion

- Media
- Business culture.

Legislation

A good start in this regard would be to consider the legislation on freedom of academic expression currently considered by the UK Parliament.

The stated purpose of the Higher Education (Freedom of Speech) Bill is "*to make provision in relation to freedom of speech and academic freedom in higher education institutions and in students' unions; and for connected purposes*".

The Bill would require a higher education provider to adopt a code of conduct that facilitates free speech and free access to the provider's places for visiting speakers.

The Bill also extends to the student unions, which would also be required to have their code of conduct.

The Office of Students (which in the UK is the institution that regulates higher education providers) would have supervisory responsibilities over the Codes of Conduct.

My view is that this is in some ways a variation on the Code of Conduct proposed in Australia by Justice French in his report on academic freedom in Australian universities. This is a good start, but it is only a partial solution to a complex issue.

Freedom of speech is much broader than academic freedom. Whilst some Australian legislation similar to the UK Bill might protect freedom of speech within academic circles, it would not extend to securing freedom of speech to the public at large.

Maybe an Ombudsman for Freedom of Expression could be considered and given a more powerful and prescriptive role than that of the present Australian Human Rights Commission.

However, this has broader politico-legal ramifications that lie outside the narrow scope of this book and would rely on the

Ombudsman to act to genuinely protect free speech. Sadly, our experience with similar bodies is that they have a left-leaning political inclination, so in some cases they merely amplify rather than act against woke attacks.

Finally, a word should be said about legislation for freedom of religious expression and belief.

Religious freedom is protected by a number of international treaties to which Australia is a signatory. For instance, the 1981 Declaration of the United Nations General Assembly states in part:

> *Art 2(1)" No one shall be subject to discrimination by any State, institution, group of persons, or person on the grounds of religion or other belief."*

> *"Art.3." Discrimination between human beings on the grounds of religion or belief constitutes an affront to human dignity and a disavowal of the principles of the Charter of the United Nations and shall be condemned as a violation of the human rights and fundamental freedoms proclaimed in the Universal Declaration of Human Rights and enunciated in detail in the International Covenants on Human Rights, and as an obstacle to friendly and peaceful relations between nations."*

> *Art. 4 (1) "All States shall take effective measures to prevent and eliminate discrimination on the grounds of religion or belief in the recognition, exercise and enjoyment of human rights and fundamental freedoms in all fields of civil, economic, political, social and cultural life."*

> *Art.4 (2)" All States shall make all effort to enact or rescind legislation where necessary to prohibit any such discrimination, and to take all appropriate measures to combat intolerance on the grounds of religion or other*

beliefs in that matter."

My concern is that the current legislative acts of Parliament in Australia do not convey clearly that freedom to practise one's own religion is both a fundamental human right and often also a tool to defending other human rights.

Current legislation seems to imply that the freedom of religious expression is granted to religious groups only by way of tolerance, more with the intent of appeasing them rather than recognising their right to practise their religion in all of life's situations. Exceptions are granted under various States' Equal Opportunity Acts more with the purpose of tolerating some practices of religious expression rather than upholding them as fundamental human rights.

Until greater recognition is given to the rights of religious persons and religious groups, we will continue to prop up religious and non-religious elements of society against one another and fail to minimise the cause and frequency of litigation between the two.

Most Australian legislation also seems to give the impression that religion is simply a set of spiritual beliefs that are taught and expressed by practising a number of specific rituals.

Although this might not be so in the case of some religions, most of them, Christianity in particular, covers much more than this. Christianity, like Islam and Sikhism, is a way of life, a whole-of-life approach based on a particular set of beliefs. Christianity is not only taught – it must also be lived. Christian beliefs are reflected in the way Christians speak, think, write, interact, work, spend their leisure time and so on.

To limit the current exceptions granted by legislation to religious bodies and religious schools only is too narrow because it ignores the large number of religious people who are confronted with challenges to their religious expression outside religious schools and churches.

I suggest, therefore, that one of the key objects of Australian equal opportunity legislation should be the protection of the human right to religious expression in **all** circumstances and to all people of faith.

Freedom of religious expression particularly underpins freedom of speech and action since much religious belief finds its practical applications outside the formal worship rituals of religious ceremonies.

Education

Education is much broader than daycare, kindergarten, school, technical college, university education and professional development.

Education is all-of-life learning. Education is what we read in the press, see on our television screens, and the music we listen to. In other words, education is culture.

Education is knowledge, but it is also appreciation of a particular viewpoint.

Whilst this book has pointed out some of the flaws inherent in our Australian curriculum, the solution to this issue is far more complex than just reforming school and university curricula.

What needs to be done is to instil in our population a renewed degree of intellectual curiosity. This means a desire to know more, to obtain more facts, to hear different viewpoints and above all, a desire to think, as opposed to just feel and experience. In brief, a desire to broaden one's horizons.

This can only be achieved if our governments and media institutions stop treating the Australian population as a people who cannot understand complex issues and, instead, start providing them with detailed arguments with pros **and** cons so they can make informed decisions.

Plenty of examples could be given, but I will just give one: climate change.

How many ordinary Australians who have taken a position on climate change, one way or another, can articulate sufficiently well the monetary and non-monetary costs of making the change away from hydrocarbons as opposed to the costs of doing nothing by 2030 or 2050? I guess very few would, and I shall not pretend to be among them.

Intellectual curiosity is not something you can instil in a person overnight. It needs to be fostered at an early age and sustained throughout life.

In the area of science, for instance, why can we not teach in our public schools the full facts of evolution and creation science? We should encourage our children to make up their minds, to become intellectually curious to discover the truth on this issue.

Educational reforms must also start by reinstating parental authority.

Until such time as we accept that parents are the primary arbiters of their children's education and that schoolteachers have only delegated parental authority, we will continue to lose control over the content our children are being taught.

Should we persist in the direction we have embarked on, our children will continue to be taught what the State wants them to be taught rather than what we, as parents, want them to learn.

I am not saying that all parents know what is good for their children, but I am also saying that the State does not know either. If different parents have different views of what is good to teach their children, at worst, we will have viewpoint diversity, which is foundational to debate, intellectual thought and freedom of speech.

On the other hand, if the State is the only arbiter of what

should be taught or allowed, then we no longer have a diversity of opinion: only one worldview prevails, and debate is dead.

Religion

I already raised the issue of religion under my remarks about legislation. However, changes need to be embraced by churches in the way in which they promote their religious beliefs.

First of all, there is a perception in some secular quarters that religion equates with loss of freedom. This is often untrue, and churches need to make this point clear.

Religion does not necessarily equate with loss of freedom. Whilst some religious practices are clearly oppressive, not all religions are the same. On the whole, most religions promote many human rights.

Michelle Bachelet, the United Nations High Commissioner for Human Rights, made the following declaration in a recent document entitled *Faith for Rights*:

> *"Human rights and faith can be mutually supportive. Indeed, many people of faith have worked at the heart of the human rights movement, precisely because of their deep attachment to respect for human dignity, human equality, and justice. "*

> *"I am convinced that faith-based actors can promote trust and respect between communities. And I am committed to assisting governments, religious authorities and civil society actors to work jointly to uphold human dignity and equality for all. "*[xxvi]

Many religions advocate humility, justice, love and mercy, but these are, in turn, the reflection of particular knowledges.

We cannot advocate humility, justice, love and mercy if we define these purely from an emotional angle. Reason needs to prevail. Reason is an important component of knowledge.

Churches need to be able to debate what is reasonable humility, reasonable justice, reasonable love and reasonable mercy.

Churches must avoid imposing their views in a dogmatic fashion and regain their place as a respected interlocutor.

Furthermore, churches must also avoid just agreeing with everything that is promoted and, in particular, they must avoid falling into the trap of Critical Race Theory.

At the same time, churches need to present the Gospel in an attractive way that addresses the cultural concerns of the day.

In an article entitled *Deconstructing Defeater Beliefs*[xxvii], leading US theologian Tim Keller informs us that Christianity needs to be presented in a way that denounces the implausibility of our current culture. He writes that Jesus must be presented as the answer to the questions the culture is asking.

In response to the issue of identity, Keller suggests the following answer:

> *"If you build your identity mainly on your class, or race or culture or performance you will necessarily vilify and disdain anyone who lacks what you consider the cornerstone of your significance … but if God is our ultimate good, then we are free to develop deep love for (what Edward calls) 'Being in general'. If we truly made the Lord our ultimate beauty and Saviour, we would have an equal love and joy in all creation, all individuals, all people groups, even in all nature and created things."*

Indeed, the Church needs to adapt its responses to the time and space culture in which it is situated. The defeater beliefs (i.e., objections to Christian beliefs) of our time are different from those of previous generations. They are also different from those currently prevailing in different cultures, for instance, in the Middle East.

We need to ascertain what these defeater beliefs are and address them in credible fashion.

Keller says we do not necessarily need to "answer" them to the fullest extent but at least deconstruct them to show that the Christian message is a viable alternative.

> *"Our purpose with these defeaters or doubts is ... to show that they are not as solid or as natural as they first appear ... it is important to show that all doubts and objections to Christianity are really alternate beliefs and faith-acts about the world ... and when you see your doubts and beliefs and ... require the same amount of evidence for them that you are asking of Christian beliefs, then it becomes evident many of them are very weak and largely adopted because of cultural pressure." (Keller).*

However, my view is that, above all, the Christian church needs to be faithful to the Scriptures. Re-inventing a new theology of the Bible in order to conform more closely to what the world advocates, the *zeitgeist*, is foolishness. To be of any value, the Church must stop trying to imitate the world and instead provide a message, a point of view, fully anchored in the truth of the Bible.

Let us start with the desire we all have (acknowledged or not) of a life beyond the grave.

Let us probe the question of whether God exists and the desire many have to acknowledge that there is a God who controls what lies beyond the grave.

Let us pose the question: Can God be anything other than purely holy? How could an unholy god be God at all if the attributes of God include purity, justice, love and compassion?

Then, let us also ask how a totally holy God could countenance having fellowship with creatures who are less than fully holy and then let us suggest the answer that is contained in the Cross: the sacrifice of the Lord Jesus Christ who paid the price to present us in the purity of His holiness to God, His heavenly Father.

The Christian church needs to go back to these basics and weave this message into the answers that meet the concerns of the present culture; principally the quest for justice and the end of all oppression.

The Christian church also needs to dispel some serious misunderstandings of its core theology. For instance, when the Scriptures refer to "submission", they do not make a dichotomy between "oppressor" and "oppressed" but rather point out how, for instance, in the case of a married couple, husband and wife serve and uphold each other, in different ways. Although the Scriptures were written in what many consider to be a "patriarchal" culture, the message of the Bible is not one where some are entitled by virtue of their position or circumstances, to "lord" over others. On the contrary, the book of James tells us that "religion that is pure and undefiled before God, the Father, is to visit orphans and widows in their affliction, and to keep oneself unstained from the world."

These are important truths. Christianity is a religion of peace, not of oppression.

Christianity is neither pro-man nor pro-woman. Christianity is pro all lives – black, white, male, female, rich and poor. Christians understand these truths and believe them but often fail to communicate them properly to the world.

Christian churches need to address this.

Most importantly, I believe Christian churches need to understand forgiveness.

In Christian circles, forgiveness is preached but not often properly practised.

The saying "churches are quick at killing their wounded" is

far too often a reflection of a judgmental approach that makes no room for forgiveness.

As a result, families are broken up, and family members become silenced and isolated.

Forgiveness is not just saying "I forgive you" and agreeing not to raise again the issue that brought about the harm and suffering; forgiveness is also a decision to renew some sort of contact or fellowship with the offender (allowing, of course, for extreme cases where this would not be realistic; for instance, in the case of rape or other chronic abuse).

The Christian Bible preaches forgiveness and highlights the forgiveness offered to sinners through the sacrifice of the Lord Jesus on the Cross of Calvary.

Jesus does not simply say: "you have expressed repentance for your wrongdoings, and you believe that I have the power to forgive you", and then leave the repentant sinner in a state of isolation, without any comfort, or sustained relationship with his Maker.

No, on the contrary, Jesus expresses His forgiveness by restoring us to Him in order to welcome us into full unity with God at the end of times.

Christian churches must, indeed, start appreciating that forgiveness implies at least some degree of willingness to restore a broken relationship. This is a key antidote to the isolation and fragmentation of our society, a key antidote to silencing conversation and destroying community.

Repentance is also essential. However, repentance can only be meaningful if it is connected to wrongdoings personally committed. One may be sorry for what our forebears did in the distant past, but this is not repentance.

Repentance is a turning-of-the-way by the individual for wrongful acts personally committed. It means that the repentant person commits to avoid repeating in the future the same actions for which he is now repenting.

Repentance is an individual act, a personal expression of regret; it can never be a group act, and this is why, as a nation, we can only say that we regret the abuses perpetrated by the early settlers, but we can never repent for them because we do not carry any responsibility for them.

Here is the point of difference with Critical Race Theory (CRT).

CRT preaches that we are responsible for what our forebears did because of our whiteness. We are all painted with the same brush, and even worst, CRT preaches that reconciliation is impossible because we are socially conditioned to be oppressors.

It is a message of despair, offering no solutions to any conflict or disagreement.

The Christian Church has a big responsibility to point out that, unlike CRT, it can offer a message of hope, a true lasting solution.

To do this, the Church needs to demonstrate two things:

1. that true repentance encourages forgiveness and

2. that true forgiveness is the precursor to reconciliation and renewed fellowship.

This is the priority for the Christian church in the 21st century.

To assist the Church in this regard, the secular world needs to appreciate that religion is not just confined to formal worship – it is also a whole way of life. This is more particularly true of the Christian faith.

Finally, the Church needs to promote true love. The present cultural mindset believes that love is shown by exerting tolerance.

This is incorrect.

Tolerating something that causes harm is not loving. We

must not tolerate the intolerable.

The challenge for the Church is to demonstrate what causes harm and how to remedy harm in a loving fashion.

To clarify: I mentioned earlier that some persons embark on a transgender experiment without knowing exactly the risks they expose themselves to, both psychologically and medically. I did say that, in the case of Nathan Verhelst, it was unloving not to have intervened in a situation that resulted in his death.

There are, however, other situations where tolerance is unloving.

For instance, drug addiction. The idea that the battle against illicit drugs cannot be won is now decades old. This is why we have needle and syringe programs (NSP) under the auspices of the Department of Health. The purpose of these programs is to prevent sexual diseases and blood-borne virus transmission.

NSP operators will undoubtedly argue that their actions are loving, but this is incorrect.

True love would show no tolerance towards drugs.

Why?

Simply because a no-tolerance policy would result in having fewer and fewer drug addicts and more and more people capable of leading functional lifestyles with all the psychological, medical and financial rewards that would result from mass rehabilitation programs.

I mention the issue of drugs and transgenderism only as examples.

There are, of course, numerous other issues confronting us. Some of these have already been raised in this book.

The challenge for the Christian Church is to engage itself in all of these cultural issues and redefine, or should I say expand, its understanding of mission.

In other words, the Church should not just aim at making converts through its works of exhortation but also at making converts through its works of application.

The job of the Church is to transform lives.

The *dunamis* of the Gospel must be demonstrated through actions relevant to the culture issues of today, with solutions that work and show true love (rather than tolerance) for a world engulfed in a devastating storm of secularisation.

To achieve this, the Church needs to extricate itself from its own culture of secularisation.

As pointed out by leading Baptist theologian Albert Mohler:

> *The moral authority of the church has been seriously buffeted by the scandal of sexual immorality that is tolerated and the scandal of sexual abuse that has been denied. The obedient church of Jesus Christ cannot just preach a biblical morality; it must live out that morality. Otherwise, our words will ring hollow.* [lxxviii]

However, this raises the issue of being permitted to live out biblical morality.

Politically, sociologically, this is becoming very difficult.

Some sections of the Christian church might be tempted to conclude that if biblical preaching is now portrayed as "hate speech", the solution is isolation, the formation of close-knit communities who live according to a specific religious order and keep to themselves. This is, of course, nothing new. Monasteries and cloisters already existed before the Reformation. Yet, this goes against the very thesis of this book, which is to engage dialogue, debate, to learn, to listen and to evaluate.

To have a dialogue, two parties are obviously required. The problem starts with the fact that the parties on the side of the woke movement have no desire to engage in a dialogue with the Church. The main reason is because the Church has lost its right to speak and cannot regain it until such time as it puts its own house in order, address its own issues, remove the splint from its own eye. This will take time and, even if this is achieved, the chances are the Church will never regain its place at the table.

Nevertheless, it would be wrong for the Church not to attempt to offer a dialogue.

Media

Our media needs to be reformed – transformed even.

The role of the media is not to tell us what to think (something it does, unfortunately, far too well and often at present). The role of the media is to inform us and encourage us to think through the issues.

The media should be asking the questions, not answering them.

The media can provide an opinion column, but it needs to give both views of the issue equal coverage, thereby encouraging the reader to think through the issue, debate it in his circle of friends or express his sentiment through a letter to the editor.

Expressions of opinion are for media consumers, not for the newspapers.

The media role is purely to facilitate the debate by providing the information in an impartial manner.

This can only happen if we encourage a new generation of editors to take this on.

Again, it assumes a mindset, nurtured during childhood, through formal and informal education, and curious to hear what the other has to say.

In particular, social media needs to accept that it is not the protector of individual sensitivities; indeed, to a very large extent, no media outlet has a right to exercise opinion censorship.

This means that the media at large needs to treat its consumers as mature adults, capable of overcoming emotional shocks.

The media needs to accept that any emotional hurt caused by the expression of a particular viewpoint is the price society has to pay to ensure that freedom of expression and democracy is preserved.

The media needs to acknowledge that freedom of speech is the paramount issue in our society and that, whilst we might be confronted with different issues, over time, each with its own specific degree of urgency, nothing is more urgent, nothing is more precious than freedom of expression.

Unless the media accepts the unsurpassable priority that must be accorded to freedom of expression, it will continue to divide, isolate and silence our present and future populations.

Business culture

Business needs to confine itself to what it does best: commercial activities.

The primary responsibility of business is to provide a financial return to its shareholders and to respect and treat its employees well.

The former part of this statement is not really contentious; the second is in the sense that viewpoints differ on what it means to treat one's employees well.

Beyond good pay and a physically safe environment, what does it mean to treat one's employees well?

It means treating them as responsible adults. Employees will come from different backgrounds, with different opinions and different levels of education.

Unless a business carries a specific charitable function grounded in a particular religious ethos or belief system, it has no right to interfere with what people say and discuss at work or in the company's social club.

We hear stories of employees losing their employment because they do not support the woke philosophy of the Board of Directors or the Chief Executive Officer. This is unacceptable in a free-thinking, tolerant and democratic country.

I made the point earlier on that a body of evidence now exists to support the view that the top corporate sector has endorsed woke philosophy in an effort to appeal to some segments of the consumer population. The view is that by doing so, one projects a more trendy, "sexy" business profile which pays off as clever marketing and improves the bottom line.

This is unacceptable, and it must be exposed.

A last word

As stated in the introductory chapter, this book is likely to be controversial. If it is, I have achieved my purpose. Not that I delight in controversy, but rather that controversy implies debate, different viewpoints and discussion.

I hope, however, that I am not misunderstood when I write that 'the most important issue we face as a nation is freedom of expression'. I do not mean by this that there should be no limitations to what we can write or say. No rights should be unfettered lest they be abused.

A great deal of commentary has been published concerning the principal piece of legislation governing freedom of expression in this country: the Racial Discrimination Act 1975 (Cwth). The legislation has attracted its fair share of criticism given the difficulty of establishing an objective test as to what is reasonably likely to offend, insult, humiliate or intimidate. This does not mean, however, that there should be no laws restricting the abuse of the right to freedom of expression.

However, given the history of laws being relied on to prevent the legitimate expression of opinions, I have strong reservations about the merits of any anti-vilification legislation.

Vilification and racial discrimination law should aim at bringing unity to our nation, but, currently, unfortunately, they seem to be used to foster division.

Furthermore, Part IIA of the Racial Discrimination Act in Australia does not apply to views expressed in private, although even that was deplored by some entrusted with protecting human rights in this country.

One of the key messages of this book is that the silence, fragility and isolation we suffer from is largely felt within the confines of our private social lives. Family members, friends, acquaintances, and colleagues cease speaking to each other; fellowship ties are severed; people "cancel" each other, and this is where the problem lies. The clans, the tribes, are decimated. Only those who espouse the same views as ours are those we assemble with. If there are any discussions in those smaller enclaves, they turn out to be more in the nature of recriminations and complaints about the status quo of our society than a stimulating exchange of opposite views about what could be done to improve it.

My principal thesis is that we cannot advance as a society without freedom of expression, without calm debate and discussion, without mutual respect for each other's opinions, intellectually as well as spiritually.

We have not got all the answers or the solutions; there is still a lot of work to be done; much to be explored; much to be discussed; much to be agreed upon.

This can only be achieved in a climate where individual human rights are respected and not merged into (or confused with) so-called group identity rights.

We must have discussions, free from emotional overtones, free from anger and resentment and accept that others may think differently without harbouring any ill feelings or hatred towards each other.

We must cease all ad hominem attacks and simply focus on the issues with humility, love and compassion for all.

Recognition of the evils perpetrated in the past is important to avoid a repetition of the same in future. The basic problem of humankind is sin. Sin is at the root of the abuse carried out throughout the ages.

Yet, resolving what happened in the past is futile: the past is past; it cannot be undone. There should be no inherited blame or guilt. The present and future are what counts.

Furthermore, the solution is not to replace past abuse with new abuse.

Abuse can take many forms. Nowadays, it is often linked with sexual predatory behaviour, but any form of oppressive domination or rejection of human dignity is also abuse.

Perversely, the woke movement practises abuse by preaching Marcuse's intolerance of the current tolerance, so, replacing one form of abuse with another.

This then creates a vicious circle that presents no opportunities for resolution.

The key to the current plague lies in open and honest debate. It means regaining the capacity to listen, to think, to ponder. It means, above all, freedom of expression, in all its forms, the right to one's opinion, the right to be heard and above all, an appreciation of the impact of what we say and do to others.

There needs to be a reversal of the loss of emotional intelligence we have suffered in the last hundred years or more

A finding of our authentic self in the rediscovery of the God of the Bible, the Creator of all who holds the key to the meaning of life.

*****

Annexure 1

Change or Suppression (Conversion) Practices Prohibition Act 2021 (Victoria)

This legislation from the Australian State of Victoria is a typical example of how freedom of expression may be curtailed by legislative fiat. It also illustrates how the persons it claims to protect can be made more vulnerable by denying them the assistance and guidance they are seeking but are not always in a position to access for themselves.

The Act deals with sexual orientation and gender identity issues.

It bans changes and suppression practices of sexual orientation and gender identity.

It defines a change or suppression practice as "a practice or conduct directed towards a person, whether with or without the person's consent—

a) on the basis of the person's sexual orientation or gender identity; and

b) for the purpose of—

    i. changing or suppressing the sexual orientation or gender identity of the person; or

    ii. inducing the person to change or suppress their sexual orientation or gender identity".

The first thing we notice in this definition is that a person who has changed his/her sexual orientation or gender identity is precluded from seeking assistance to revert to his/her biological identity.

In other words, the Act assists transitioners but not detransitioners.

It does not respect the fact that a person may change her mind.

It bans all forms of psychological, psychiatric or other therapy intervention for what is actually a mental illness.

It bans prayers or other religious practices destined to suppress sexual orientation again whether requested or not.

It prohibits moving a person outside of Victoria for the purpose of changing or suppressing the sexual orientation or gender identity of the person, whether this is at the request of the person concerned or not.

The Victorian Equal Opportunity and Human Rights Commission has the right to prosecute offences committed under the Act.

A Canberra-based specialist human rights legal firm, Human Rights Law Alliance, has pointed out that the legislation stands in contradiction with the provisions made in another Victorian piece of legislation, the Charter of Rights and Responsibilities Victoria.

In particular, it pointed out that the legislation "discriminates in favour of gender transition treatments that involve experimental chemical and hormone treatments" and that it "fails to protect children from being exposed to the dangerous effects of procedures when they are incapable of giving informed consent."

*****

Bibliography

Books

Allen S.D. *Why Social Justice is not Biblical Justice*, Credo House Publishers,2020.

Babones, S *The New Authoritarianism*, Polity Press 2018

Baucham V.T, Jnr. *Fault Lines* Salem Books, 2021

Bruckner *An Imaginary Racism, Islamophobia and Guilt*, Polity Press, English translation 2018

Bruckner P. *The Tyranny of Guilt*, Princeton University Press, English translation, 2010

Campbell B & Manning J. *The Rise of Victimhood Culture*, Palgrave McMillan. 2018.

Chavura C et al, Reason, *Religion & the Australian Polity, A Secular State?* Routledge, 2019

Crouch A. *Culture Making, Recovering our Creative Calling*, Intervarsity Press, 2008

Crouch A *Playing God, Redeeming the Gift of Power*, Intervarsity Press, 2013

Evans C & Stone A, *Open Minds, Academic Freedom and Freedom of Speech in Australia*, La Trobe University Press, 2021

Furedi F. *How Fear Works, Culture of Fear in the 21st century*, Bloomsbury, 2018

Furedi F. *Why Border Matters*, Routledge 2021

Furedi F. *100 Years of Identity Crisis, Culture War over Socialisation* de Gruyter, 2021

Furedi F, *Where Have All the Intellectuals Gone (2nd ed)* Bloomsbury 2004

Goldsworthy J, *Losing Faith in Democracy*, Quadrant May 2015

Gooding D & Lennox J, *Being Truly Human*, Myrtlefield Trust, *2018*

Hanson V.D, *The Dying Citizen*, Hachette, 2021

Haidt J, *The Righteous Mind*, Penguin Books, 2013

Harari Y.N. *Homo Deus, A Brief History of Tomorrow*, Harper Collins, 2015

Hicks R.C. *Explaining Postmodernism*, Connor Court Publishing 2019

Hirsch E.D, Jnr, *Why Knowledge Matters*, Harvard University Press, 2016

Jacobs. *How to Think, A Guide for the Perplexed*, Profile Books, 2018

Jones B. *What is to be done, Political Engagement & Saving the Planet*, Scribe, 2020

Jones D.M *History's Fools, The Pursuit of Idealism and the Revenge of Politics; Oxford University Press, 2020*

Keller T. *Making Sense of God*, Hodder & Stoughton, 2016

Keller T, *The Reason for God, Belief in an Age of Scepticism*, Hodder & Stoughton, 2009

Koop E & Schaeffer F, *Whatever Happened to the Human Race*, Crossway,1983

Koukl G. *Tactics*, Zondervan, 2009

Lennox J.C, *2084: Artificial Intelligence and The Future of Humanity*, Zondervan 2020

Lake M, *The Bible in Australia*, New South Publishing 2020

Lukianoff G.& Haidt J, *The Coddling of the American Mind*, Penguin Books, 2018

Mies M & Shiva V, *Ecofeminism*, Zedbooks 2014

Modood T. *Multiculturalism*, second edition, Polity Press 2013

Mohler A.R Jr, *The Gathering Storm*, Nelson Books, 2020

Murray D, *The Strange Death of Europe*, Bloomsbury, 2017

Murray D, *The Madness of Crowds, Gender, Race & Identity*, Bloomsbury, 2019

Murray D, *The War on the West*, Harper Collins, 2022

Peterson, J.G. *Beyond Order, 12 More Rules for Life,* Penguin Books, 2021

Piper J, *Bloodlines, Race, Cross & The Christian,* Crossway, 2011

Pluckrose H & Lindsay J, *Cynical Theories.* Pitchstone, 2020

Rauch J, *Kindly Inquisitors, The New Attacks on Free Thought,* University of Chicago, 2013

Rhodes C, *Woke Capitalism, How Corporate Morality is Sabotaging Democracy,* Bristol University Press, 2022

Rothman S, *The End of the Experiment,* Routledge 2017

Schaeffer F.A, *Escape from Reason,* Intervarsity Press, 1968.

Schaeffer, F.A, *A Christian Manifesto,* Crossway Books, 1982

Shellenberger M. *Apocalypse Never,* Harper Collins, 2020

Shorter A, *Multiculturalism,* Polity Press 2022

Shrier A, *Irreversible Damage,* Swift 2020

Strachan O, *Christianity & Wokeness,* Salem Books, 2021

Taylor C, *A Secular Age,* Harvard University Press, 2007

Thrupp J, Ed. *Australia Tomorrow,* Connor Court Publishing, 2021

Trueman C. *The Rise and Triumph of the Modern Self,* Crossway, 2020

Watkin C, *Michel Foucault,* P&R Publishing, 2018

Watkin, C, *Gilles Deleuze,* P&R Publishing 2020

Parliament of Australia, Racial Discrimination Act 1975 (Cwth)

Articles and Journals

- The Weekend Australian, *Ideology strangles courses at unis"*, 16-17 January 2021
- The Weekend Australian, *Human factor means juries fallible but we defend system for democracy's sake,* January 15, 2022
- The Weekend Australian, *Funding threat to the memory of our nation,* June 12-13, 2021.
- Quincy Bell an A V Tavistock and Portman NHS Trust and others (2020) EWHC 3272 (Admin) 1 December 2020, Summary Judgment, Judiciary of England & Wales,
- Bernard Lane, *Gender Ideologues' Alarming Campaign to Get Kids While They're Young,* Quillette, 29 March 2022.
- Guide to supporting a student to affirm or transition gender identity at school, https://studentwellbeinghub.edu.au/media/9548/guide-to-supporting-a-student-to-affirm-or-transition-gender-identity-at-school_oct-2015.pdf; accessed 5/04/2022
- https://www.researchgate.net/publication/341550995_The_Tendency_to_Feel_Victimized_in_Interpersonal_and_Intergroup_Relationships
- Scott Barry Kaufman, Unravelling the Mindset of Victimhood; The Scientific American, June 29, 2020 https://www.researchgate.net/publication/317777288_Perpetual_ingroup_victimhood_as_a_distorted_lens_Effects_on_attribution_and_categorization
- Harding Susan. "Representing Fundamentalism: The Problem of the Repugnant Cultural Other." *Social*

Research, vol. 58, no. 2, 1991, pp. 373–393. *JSTOR*, www.jstor.org/stable/40970650. Accessed 21 July 2021.

- Williamson V, Murphy D, Greenberg N. COVID-19 and experiences of moral injury in front-line key workers. *Occup Med (Lond).* 2020;70(5):317-319. doi:10.1093/occmed/kqaa052

- Human Rights Law Alliance, *The process as punishment, the misuse of vilification laws,* https://hrla.org.au/the-process-as-punishment-the-misuse-of-vilification-laws/; accessed 29/09/2011

- Gemma Tognini, *Like Chamberlain, we are attempting to appease monsters,* The Australian, November 6-7, 2021

- *Facebook blackout put lives in danger,* the Weekend Australian, May 7-8, 2022

- Ben Jensen, *"Fighting the classroom crisis with data for good measure,* The Weekend Australian. June 19-20, 2021

- Noel Pearson, *Schools paper ends teaching debate once and for always"* The Weekend Australian, August14-15 2021

- John Sweller, *why inquiry-based approaches harm students 'learning,* Centre for Independent Studies, Analysis Paper 24, August 2021.

- Institute of Public Affairs, IPA National Curriculum submission, 2021.

- Natasha Bita, *National curriculum goes all old school for a modern age*; The Weekend Australian, May14-14 2022

- Janet Albrechtsen, *"O-Week censors excel themselves",* The Weekend Australian, March 14-15, 2020

- Free speech crisis at Australian Universities confirmed by new research, Institute of Public Affairs, media release, August 31 2019, https://ipa.org.au/publications-ipa/media-releases/free-speech-crisis-at-australias-universities-confirmed-by-new-research, accessed 7/12/2021

- Hon. Justice French, Report of the Independent Review of Freedom of Speech in Australian Higher Education Providers, March 2019

- Tim Keller, *Deconstructing Defeater Beliefs, Leading the Secular to Christ*, https://firstpresaugusta.org/wp-content/uploads/2019/06/Deconstructing-Defeater-Beliefs.Tim-Keller.pdf (accessed 31.05.2022).

References and End Notes

Introduction

[i] Frank Furedi, *Where have all the intellectuals gone*, Bloomsbury 2004

[ii] Jonathan Haidt, *The Righteous Mind, Why Good People and Divided by Politics and Religion*, Penguin Books 2013

[iii] As reported in the Weekend Australian January 16-17, 2021, "Ideology strangles courses at unis." The article also stated that a mere quarter of English literature subjects involved the study of great works and that in the political sciences, only 10 per cent of subjects offered taught students about the history and political thought. Freedom, a key tenet of the study of social sciences was also found in only just 10 per cent of 524 possible subjects.

[iv] Douglas Murray, *The Madness of Crowds, Gender, Race and Identity*, Bloomsbury, *2019, p. 116*

[v] As quoted in *Cynical Theories*, Helen Pluckrose & James Lindsay, Swift (2020). p 206

Chapter 1

[vi] Ibid, p.42

[vii] In fact, this view has already been advocated for some time by Peter Singer who is Professor of Bioethics at Princeton University. Singer does not believe in human exceptionalism; in other words, we are not different from animals, we have no more value than a chimpanzee or a horse. Furthermore, Singer makes a difference between a human being and a person and to be a person, one must be capable of making decisions, hence the foetus is not a person, nor is the severally mentally impaired or those who are suffering from advanced dementia.

[viii] Frank Furedi, Why Borders Matter, why humanity must relearn the art of drawing boundaries, Routledge, 2021

[ix] https://www.helpguide.org/articles/mental-health/emotional-intelligence-eq.htm

Chapter 2
[x] The Rise and Triumph of the Modern Self, Carl Trueman, Crossway,2020
[xi] Human factor means juries fallible but we defend system for democracy's sake, Janet Albrechtsen, The Week End Australian, January 15, 2022
[xii] Frank Furedi, *The short story is they are coming for the classics, the* Weekend Australian, October 16-17, 2021.
[xiii] Gideon Haigh, *Funding threat to the memory of our nation*, The Weekend Australian, June 12-13, 2021.
[xiv] Summary Judgment, Judiciary of England @ Wales, Quincy Bell an A v Tavistock and Portman NHS Trust and others (2020) EWHC 3272 (Admin) 1 December 2020
[xvxv] Douglas Murray, op.cit, p.184
[xvi] *When the pressure to change wins over,* The Weekend Australian, August 20-21, 2022.
[xvii] Bernard Lane, *Gender Ideologues' Alarming Campaign to Get Kids While They're Young,* Quillette, 29 March 2022.
[xviii] Guide to supporting a student to affirm or transition gender identity at school,
https://studentwellbeinghub.edu.au/media/9548/guide-to-supporting-a-student-to-affirm-or-transition-gender-identity-at-school_oct-2015.pdf; accessed 5/04/2022

Chapter 3
[xix] Stephen R.C. Hicks, Explaining Modernism, Skepticism and Socialism from Rousseau to Foucault, Connor Court Publishing, 2019.
[xx] Ibid, p.23.
[xxi] Ibid, p.39
[xxii] Ibid, p.49
[xxiii] Ibid, p. 82.
[xxiv] Carl Trueman, op.cit. p.204

xxv Sigmund Freud, Civilisation and its Discontents, trans. James Strachey (New York: W.W Norton, 1989, as quoted by Carl Trueman, ibid. p.205
xxvi ibid p.221

Chapter 4
xxvii https://www.thearda.com/timeline/events/event_46.asp
xxviii Haidt (2013), op.cit. p.349
xxix The Forgotten People, Rt Hon R.G Menzies, 22 May 1942, https://www.timnicholls.com.au/forgotten_people

Chapter 5
xxx The Rise of Victimhood Culture, Campbell & Manning, Palgrave Macmillan 2018.
xxxi Ibid, p. 13
xxxii Ibid, p. 14
xxxiii
https://www.researchgate.net/publication/341550995_The_Tendency_to_Feel_Victimized_in_Interpersonal_and_Intergroup_Relationships
xxxiv Scott Barry Kaufman, Unravelling the Mindset of Victimhood; The Scientific American, June 29, 2020
xxxv
https://www.researchgate.net/publication/317777288_Perpetual_ingroup_victimhood_as_a_distorted_lens_Effects_on_attribution_and_categorization
xxxvi Harding, Susan. "Representing Fundamentalism: The Problem of the Repugnant Cultural Other." *Social Research*, vol. 58, no. 2, 1991, pp. 373–393. *JSTOR*, www.jstor.org/stable/40970650. Accessed 21 July 2021.
xxxvii Campbell & Manning, op.cit. p.88
xxxviii Abigail Shrier, Irreversible Damage, Teenage Girls and the Transgender Craze, Swift Press, 2021, p.44-57.
xxxix Ibid, p.53.
xl Williamson V, Murphy D, Greenberg N. COVID-19 and experiences of moral injury in front-line key workers. *Occup Med (Lond)*. 2020;70(5):317-319. doi:10.1093/occmed/kqaa052

Chapter 6

[xli] Frank Furedi "How Fear Works; Culture of Fear in the 21st century, Bloomsbury 2018, p.144

[xlii] Ibid, p.238

[xliii] Greg Lukianoff & Jonathan Haidt, *The Coddling of the American Mind,* Penguin Books, 2019, p.167.

[xliv] Ibid, p. 171

[xlv] Human Rights Law Alliance, *The process as punishment, the misuse of vilification laws, https://hrla.org.au/the-process-as-punishment-the-misuse-of-vilification-laws/;* accessed 29/09/2011

[xlvi] Campbell & Manning, op.cit. p 148.

[xlvii] Extracted from Voddie T. Baucham Jr. *Fault lines, the social justice movement and evangelicalism's looming catastrophe",* Salem Books 2021, p.70.

Chapter 7

[xlviii] Ibid, p.69-79.

[xlix] Gemma Tognini, *Like Chamberlain, we are attempting to appease monsters,* The Australian, November 6-7, 2021.

[l] RAND Corporation, Santa Monica, Calif. *Truth Decay,* Copyright 2018 RAND Corporation

[li] Wilding, D., Fray, P., Molitorisz, S. & McKewon, E. 2018, *The Impact of Digital Platforms on News and Journalistic Content,* University of Technology Sydney, NSW.

[lii] Menzies Research Centre 2021, *SOS Strengthening Online Safety, Empowering Australian Parents to Keep their Children Safe Online,*

[liii] Ibid, p.13

[liv] Facebook blackout put lives in danger, the Week End Australian, May 7-8, 2022, p. 5

[lv] The Weed End Australian, May 14-15, 2022, p.25

[lvi] Douglas Murray, The War on the West, how to prevail in the age of unreason, Harper Collins. 2022 p.62

[lvii] *"Action Now, Classroom Ready Teachers"* Teacher Education Advisory Group, Dec. 2014

[lviii] https://www.sstuwa.org.au/research/question-mark-over-accuracy-and-reliability-pisa-tests

[lix] As reported by the Menzies Research Centre in its July 2021 submission to ACARA on the issue of the review of the Australian curriculum

[lx] Ben Jensen, "Fighting the classroom crisis with data for good measure, The Weekend Australian. June 19-20, 2021

[lxilxi] The War of the Roses was fought between 1455 and 1485 between the Houses of York and Lancaster in a bid to access the English throne

[lxii] Noel Pearson, *Schools paper ends teaching debate once and for always"* The Weekend Australian, August14-15 2021

[lxiii] John Sweller, *why inquiry-based approaches harm students' learning,* Centre for Independent Studies, Analysis Paper 24, August 2021.

[lxiv] Institute of Public Affairs, IPA National Curriculum submission, 2021.

[lxv] Janet Albrechtsen, *"O-Week censors excel themselves",* The Weekend Australian, March 14-15, 2020

[lxvi] Free speech crisis at Australian Universities confirmed by new research, Institute of Public Affairs, media release, August 31 2019, https://ipa.org.au/publications-ipa/media-releases/free-speech-crisis-at-australias-universities-confirmed-by-new-research, accessed 7/12/2021

[lxvii] Hon. Justice French, Report of the Independent Review of Freedom of Speech in Australian Higher Education Providers, March 2019

[lxviii] Carl Rhodes, *Woke Capitalism, how corporate morality is sabotaging democracy,* Bristol University Press, 2022a

[lxix] The Week End Australian, April 16-17, 2022, p.17

[lxx] Douglas Murray, The War on the West, how to prevail in the age of unreason, Harper Collins, 2022, p.66

[lxxi] See Wikipedia, https://en.wikipedia.org/wiki/D%27Hondt_method#Example

Chapter 8

[lxxii] *Marcuse, Herbert (1969). "Repressive Tolerance". A Critique of Pure Tolerance. Boston: Beacon Press., p.109*

[lxxiii] Institute for Civil Society, http://www.i4cs.com.au/author/marks/, sourced 25/4/2022

Chapter 9

[lxxiv] "Forget Multiculturalism:, Dave Pellowe The Spectator, 20/90/2002, https://www.spectator.com.au/2022/09/forget-multiculturalism/ (sourced 21/11/2022)

lxxv Augusto Zimmermann," Australia's miracle of multiculturalism", Spectator Australia, 03/09/2022, sourced on 21/11/2022

Chapter 10

lxxvi

https://www.ohchr.org/EN/Issues/FreedomReligion/Pages/FaithForRights.aspx (accessed 23.9.2021)

lxxviilxxvii Tim Keller, Deconstructing Defeater Beliefs, Leading the Secular to Christ, https://firstpresaugusta.org/wp-content/uploads/2019/06/Deconstructing-Defeater-Beliefs.Tim-Keller.pdf (accessed 31.05.2022)

lxxviii R. Albert Mohler Jr. The Gathering Storm, Secularism, Culture and the Church, Nelson Books,2020/

About the Author

Philippe Jaquenod, a father of three adult children, made Australia his home fifty years ago when he arrived in Sydney as a young adult. Now living in Western Australia. Philippe has a rich background in social activism, business, finance, and political research. He holds a Bachelor of Arts from Macquarie University and is an Australian-accredited translator in the French and English languages.